DIGITAL CHARACTER PAINTING USING PHOTOSHOP® CS3

DON SEEGMILLER

CHARLES RIVER MEDIA

Boston, Massachusetts

Publisher and General Manager, Charles River Media: Stacy L. Hiquet

Associate Director of Marketing: Sarah O'Donnell

Manager of Editorial Services: Heather Talbot

Marketing Manager: Jordan Casey

Marketing Assistant: Adena Flitt

Project Editor: Karen A. Gill

Technical Reviewer: Howard Lyon

CRM Editorial Services Coordinator: Jennifer Blaney

Copy Editor: Ruth Saavedra

Interior Layout Tech: Judy Littlefield

Cover Designer: Tyler Creative

Cover Images: Don Seegmiller

CD-ROM Producer: Brandon Penticuff

Indexer: Valerie Perry

Proofreader: Melba Hopper

Charles River Media, Inc.
25 Thomson Place
Boston, MA 02210
617-757-7900
617-757-7969 (fax)
info@charlesriver.com
www.charlesriver.com

This book is printed on acid-free paper.

Don Seegmiller. *Digital Character Painting Using Photoshop CS3.*
ISBN-10: 1-58450-533-8
ISBN-13: 978-1-58450-533-4
Library of Congress Catalog Card Number: 2007931939
All brand names and product names mentioned in this book are trademarks or service marks of their respective companies. Any omission or misuse (of any kind) of service marks or trademarks should not be regarded as intent to infringe on the property of others. The publisher recognizes and respects all marks used by companies, manufacturers, and developers as a means to distinguish their products.

Printed in Canada
08 09 10 11 12 TC 10 9 8 7 6 5 4 3 2 1

Charles River Media titles are available for site license or bulk purchase by institutions, user groups, corporations, etc. For additional information, please contact the Special Sales Department at 800-347-7707.

Requests for replacement of a defective CD-ROM must be accompanied by the original disc, your mailing address, telephone number, date of purchase, and purchase price. Please state the nature of the problem, and send the information to Charles River Media, Inc., 25 Thomson Place, Boston, MA 02210. CRM's sole obligation to the purchaser is to replace the disc, based on defective materials or faulty workmanship, but not on the operation or functionality of the product.

This book is dedicated to my family;
in particular, Marti, my dear wife,
who has always helped keep my vision clear
and my perspective correct.

CONTENTS

ACKNOWLEDGMENTS

I would like to thank everyone who has had an influence on my development as an artist but, unfortunately, there is not room to list each name. However, there are a few who stand out and need mentioning. First, my wife Marti, who is so patient with me and took the chance that marrying an artist would not mean living in a shack while I pondered my next masterpiece. My children Jennifer, Nicole, and Andrew, who learned early on that tasting paint was not a good thing. My parents, for their support. My students, who teach me as much as I teach them. Howard, for being a good friend and not tearing the book apart too much as he reviewed it. Karen, for her gentle patience while heading this project. And all those at Thomson, who helped make sense of my rambling and created a gorgeous book. Thank you again, everyone.

ABOUT THE AUTHOR

Don Seegmiller has been an artist as long as he can remember. Some of his earliest memories are of getting into trouble in school because he was drawing pictures in the margins on his math pages instead of doing the addition and subtraction.

In 1973, he was accepted into the art department at Brigham Young University on scholarship. As with most artists, academics were of secondary importance to the drawn image, yet, in the spring of 1979, he did graduate with a Bachelor of Fine Arts degree in graphic design, with a specialization in illustration. He was promptly employed by one of the departments at the school as a graphic designer/illustrator. While employed at Brigham Young University, he decided that commercial deadlines were not what he wanted to be dealing with, so he became a fine artist. He began to paint egg tempera paintings in the evenings, and, after trying various subject matter, decided that his heart and talent were most at home with the human figure. In the fall of 1980, with three paintings under his arm, he traveled to Santa Fe, New Mexico, seeking representation in one of the many art galleries in town. His work has been shown in Wadle Galleries of Santa Fe since 1981. He has painted more than 500 oil paintings of the figure and is represented in public and private collections worldwide.

In the spring of 1995, two opportunities that could not be ignored presented themselves. Don was asked to teach figure drawing at Brigham Young University for both the fine arts department and the graphics department. Since that time, the departments have merged, and he continues to teach senior-level illustration, traditional head painting, figure drawing, and digital painting for the department of visual design. He also joined the staff of Saffire Corporation, where he was the art director for six years. Saffire was a small developer of video games for publishers such as Nintendo, Electronic Arts, Titus, and Mindscape. Don continues to be active in game development with clients such as Microsoft, Wizards of the Coast, and Bethesda Software.

Don is a regular speaker at the Game Developers Conference. In the spring of 2002, 2003, 2004, and 2005, he did full-day tutorials on character design and digital painting and creativity.

Don was the keynote speaker at the Association of Medical Illustrators convention in New Orleans in the summer of 2003 and continues to teach workshops at their annual convention. He has taught workshops at individual game developers conventions around the country. He also has taught at the University of California, Irvine extension, and the Ringling School of Art in Sarasota, Florida, and the Art Institute of California San Diego. He teaches online workshops for the CG Society and writes and teaches online courses for The Academy of Art University in San Francisco.

Don traveled for a while demonstrating Metacreations Painter 6, 7, 8, 9, and 10 at the major trade shows. His work is featured in *The Painter 6 Wow! Book*, *The Painter 7 Wow! Book*, *The Painter 8 Wow! Book*, *The Painter 9 Wow! Book*, *Electronic Step by Step Design*, *Spectrum 7*, and *Spectrum 8*, and he was a judge for Ballistic Media's *Painter* book.

Don continues to pursue his traditional fine art, digital art, character design, and teaching passions.

PREFACE

Why strive to be an artist? There are certainly easier ways to make a living, and there are definitely better paying vocations. Combine those two points with the fact that most artists are not at all satisfied with the results of their efforts, and the question almost becomes absurd. Why on earth would anyone want to do this? Why does someone continue with an activity or profession when a sense of failure or disappointment with the final product is so common? If you were an air traffic controller or surgeon and failed to reach your goal at the end of each landing or surgery, I doubt you could continue in that profession. Why, then, do we keep trying to do this? I really think that there is only one reason that we persevere in our efforts: We love the feeling that the process of creating art instills within us. It is the travel and not the destination that we love. Professional artists or not, we feel the same inner reward when we are in the process of creating art, and this alone is reason enough to continue to struggle and call ourselves artists.

I myself am an artist through and through. I just cannot seem to control myself. Give me a crayon at a restaurant, and I will draw on the tablecloth. I carry a sketchbook with me always. My hands permanently smell like turpentine. For as long as I can remember, this need to draw and paint has been part of my existence. As for a label, you may call me a professional artist in as much as creating art is how I support my family and lifestyle. Up until 1995, I was only a "traditional" artist. I painted in oil and sold the paintings through a traditional art gallery. Never had I seriously considered the possibility of doing art on a computer, and yet I remember vividly in the late 1970s going into an art supply store and seeing a massive machine in the corner. It was a computer, and the darn thing could make pictures. As I look back, the pictures were not very sophisticated, being mostly primitive shapes filled with colors or gradients, and the output was on Polaroid film. Nevertheless, it did not matter that the machine was as big as a small car or that it cost as much as a small house. I was hooked on digital art. The possibilities seemed endless.

Here it is a new millennium. Computers are small enough to be easily carried when you are traveling, imaging programs have now reached a level where virtually anything is possible, and movies, games, the Internet, television, and even the printed media are relying more and more on digital imagery to communicate ideas. It is now economically possible for artists of all experience levels to create digital content, and as an audience, we are becoming more sophisticated in our demands on the quality of images we see. The future of art is here whether you like it or not.

So what does all this philosophy have to do with a book on character design and digital art? Plenty, I hope. What you have in your hands is my attempt to merge two distinct yet intimately interrelated subjects: character design and digital painting.

Character design is all about ideas and how to put those ideas together. Any time that you need to design a character, your mind starts spinning and the cogs start turning. You come up with ideas that will fulfill the client's vision but that are also merged with your thoughts and ideas. Possibly you are lucky and you only have to come up with ideas for yourself. Your ideas may be very concrete or amorphous. It really does not matter who you are designing for; the design process is all about ideas.

On the other hand, the digital painting process is about the combination of method, techniques, and artistic theory. It is all about how to do a "thing," and that thing is how to make something that is ultimately viewed in two dimensions imitate three dimensions. The subject is not only about the theory of how to make images in two dimensions but often how to create a specific effect in a specific application.

This book is about merging these two distinct subjects. Though different, neither of these subjects—character design and digital painting—can stand on its own. A great design is nothing if you can't communicate that idea to the audience; conversely, the most beautifully rendered image is nothing without a good idea.

This is the crux and solution to the problem at hand. Why not have a book that deals with both subjects? The first section could explain how to come up with great ideas, and the second could explain how to visualize those ideas so that others could appreciate their beauty. So here is that attempt at merging two very creative and different disciplines that nevertheless require each other to be successful.

The book is in three parts. Part I deals with character design and coming up with the ideas that are worth visualizing. Part II is a brief review of some traditional artistic principles that will improve your art skills when you incorporate them into digital painting. Part III shows you how to solve some of the visual problems that will always be present when you are painting digital art.

There is only one reason for this book, and that is to help you merge the differing disciplines of character design, the ever-expanding digital universe, and good old-fashioned artistic skill and creativity. This book has been written so that anyone from the seasoned professional to the aspiring artist will find something of use. Professionals will possibly find ideas for ways of doing things that had never occurred to them before. Aspiring artists will find valuable information on basic artistic principles and specific techniques for designing a character. If you are neither a professional nor an aspiring artist, I hope that there is some art you will find intriguing to look at.

I found it rather difficult to write a book about the technique of digital art and how it merges with traditional principles because there is no definitive right or wrong way to create art. Almost everything that you find here is a result of my study and experience as a professional artist since the early 1980s. The artistic ideas presented are for the most part not new but rather are as old as art itself. I have found that, while artists have been taught the same basic principles, sometimes the implementation of that knowledge is less well taught.

I hope that you gain some insight into the creative process as well as some additional skills while you paint.

INTRODUCTION

Have you ever doodled creatures on the edges of the phone book while waiting for directory assistance? How many of you have scribbled on a scrap of paper while sitting in a boring meeting?

I would venture to say that almost everyone has at one time or another spent some time drawing the characters and monsters that populate our minds. For a few of us, this random doodling begins to become something more. We take these random images and expand on them until they are more fully realized. For an even smaller number, this drawing becomes a painting. For some, this compulsion to draw and paint the population of our mind ultimately becomes, if not our vocation, then an activity that we feel almost an obsession to engage in.

This book is for all people who have ever felt the need to put the images in their heads down into a more solid statement to share with others. There is something in this book for you whether you are a complete novice wondering where to begin to draw the characters of your imagination, or whether you are a seasoned professional looking for information to help improve your current skills.

The book is divided into three basic parts. Part I deals with ideas and is about things of a more cerebral nature. It covers such topics as how to get ideas and how to get them out so that others may see them. It serves as an outline for a method of turning on the tap in your brain and letting the ideas flow and develop. Artists of all levels should understand the chapters in this part.

Part II is about artistic fundamentals that will help you take your ideas to the next step: drawing and painting them so that others may appreciate your efforts. This part is laid out somewhat like a textbook and specifically focuses on things that seem difficult for both beginning and more advanced artists in their struggles with drawing and painting. In most areas, a basic understanding of artistic principles is not needed. Most subjects are covered so that both the beginning and more advanced artist will understand the concepts.

Part III is a series of tutorials that show how I have handled different subject matter when drawing and painting. This part does not give you an exact formula for duplicating what you are seeing but allows you to work along through the creation process and then use what you have learned in your own work. These tutorials contain completely new material.

SOFTWARE AND HARDWARE REQUIREMENTS

This is a book on digital painting, so you need certain equipment to follow the demonstrations and exercises. You obviously need a computer with lots of hard drive space as well as a monitor capable of displaying at least 24-bit color. You will have greater success if you use some sort of stylus when painting. Painting with a mouse is possible but feels a lot like painting with a bar of soap.

As for software, I'm using Photoshop CS3. It's assumed that you have a fundamental understanding of this software. If you do not have Photoshop CS3, Photoshop CS2, Photoshop CS, or Photoshop 7 will suffice. Earlier versions of Photoshop are not recommended, as the brush engine in later versions was significantly improved over earlier versions. In Part III, where the tutorials appear, great detail on how to achieve a particular effect is not necessarily provided since this is not a Photoshop "how-to" section. Rather, Part III is more about getting into my brain and watching the process as each painting is completed.

Many other 2D applications will suffice if you do not own Photoshop CS3. Be aware that you will not be able to reproduce the effects exactly, but you will be able to use the general principles discussed.

It is my hope that this book will serve you as you strive to be a better character designer and artist.

CHARACTER DESIGN

A section of a book that is dedicated to character design is an unusual thing. Many books have had individual chapters that mention some aspect of character design, and some even go as far as having a few images supporting the text. This book is different. Part I of this book will give the reader a list of questions that every character designer must consider as they begin to create. Without considering all of these ideas, a character may be very creative, but if it does not fit the needs of the project, then time has been wasted. Not only does this part pose the questions you must ask yourself as a character designer, but these chapters will give you some clear, concise, and creative methods for coming up with and improving your designs. Once you have the ideas, we'll explore how to improve on them and give your character a life of its own. Combine all these things, and you, the reader, will have an arsenal of information and exercises never before presented in one volume.

As you go through Part I, try to use and remember some of this information as you create. Your character designs will be better for it.

INTRODUCTION TO CHARACTER DESIGN

For as long as people have been telling stories (and, eventually, writing books), they have verbally and with the written word created different characters to populate their fictional worlds. The beauty and strength of many of these character descriptions are that much was left up to the listener's or reader's imagination. With the advent of television, movies, and now video games, however, things have changed. The medium is visually describing the characters and environments for us as an audience. While our perceptions will still be unique to each of us, those perceptions are now closer together than they have ever been.

As an audience, we are getting more sophisticated in our expectations of visual imagery. When we were children, Frankenstein (Figure 1.1) was quite terrifying. We had probably never seen such a frightening creature, and none of our childhood experiences could have caused us to imagine anything like it. The movie was trying to take over our imagination and make us see exactly what it wanted us to see.

FIGURE 1.1   The Frankenstein monster.

Eventually, as we grew up, those creatures were no longer as frightening, and we wanted more scare for our movie dollar. In the late 1970s, *Star Wars* was released. Here was a whole universe based on one man's vision, and he wanted us to see exactly what he wanted us to see. To a large degree he succeeded, because we all know what Darth Vader looks like, and we all equate him with evil. The desire of creators to have us see their individual vision carries on to this day in movies like *Tomb Raider*, where there is very little room for the leading actress to add to the character's personality. We already know what Laura Croft looks and acts like. Some of these characters are so strong that they actually become cultural icons. The original Frankenstein is a good example of a character's staying power.

Nowadays, there is less room for our imagination to create unique images within our heads when we are presented with such visually stunning creations. Increasingly, characters are so well designed that the images and ideas they convey are relatively the same regardless of each viewer's background.

With this power to take over another's imagination for a short time comes a responsibility to do it well. You do not want to be remembered as the character designer of one of the silliest characters to ever grace the screen or monitor; you'd like to be renowned for creating one of the most memorable ones. Think back on some of the movies with characters that enthralled and disappointed you when you were younger. They could have scared you nearly to death, sent your imagination soaring, or seemed so ridiculous that you were either disappointed or bored. We all have our favorites. Some characters that had excellent character designs were those in the movies *Dark Crystal*, *Labyrinth*, and *Alien*, among many others.

On the other hand, there is a movie called *Robot Monster*, made way back in 1953. The main creature in the movie was a man in a gorilla suit who was wearing what looked like a cardboard, old-fashioned diving helmet, with car antennas glued to the side. It looked something like Figure 1.2.

FIGURE 1.2   The "Robot Monster" sketch.

It is so ridiculous that you can't help but laugh. This is definitely an example of bad character design.

Very little has been written on what direction you should take when designing characters for the screen, games, and print. This may very well be because we are so individual that it is hard to quantify what makes a good character. What is good character design for one individual may not be for another. Most of the character-design process itself is based on rather ambiguous ideas of what is creative and what is not.

Have no doubt: character design is an art. The fleshing-out of a character is successful to a large degree when you apply traditional artistic principles to a creative idea. Most of us who desire to work in the entertainment industry (whether in film, games, or something else) are just expected to know how to flesh out a character when we graduate from school. In addition, most of us just assume that because we can draw a dragon or an elf, we are character designers. After all, we have been drawing monsters, villains, soldiers, and heroes for as long as we can remember. The sad fact is, however, that artists, even good ones, are not necessarily good character designers.

Like all of the arts, character design has its own set of fundamental skills that if mastered will make artists better designers. Until very recently, most art schools did not offer a curriculum that dealt with the basics associated with good character design. This area is often overlooked in schools, possibly because, as with many of the arts, there is no one way of doing something correctly in character design (as there is, say, in chemistry). The problem with this approach is that artists are left to their own devices to figure out their own working methods. This approach may work for some, but most of the time, artists spend a lot of wasted time and effort exploring dead-end avenues, and for many, there is no success without direction.

Most students want a set of rules or techniques that they can work on mastering. After mastering the basic skills, they then have more freedom to accept the premises taught, or they can reject them and explore their own directions. Almost always, success is quicker when you know and can work with some fundamental ideas.

For this reason, this section presents a series of "basic rules" that, if used, will improve your abilities as a character designer. Most of the ideas are not original in and of themselves. The uniqueness of this section lies in the fact that the ideas have rarely been combined into one section on character design.

WHAT IS CHARACTER DESIGN?

What is good character design? For that matter, what is character design? The art of character design is no more and no less than creating someone or something that, taken in the context of its environment, will elicit a belief, reaction, or expectation from the audience about the physical makeup, disposition, and personality of the creation. Why, then, is there such a wide diversity of good and bad character design when the premise is so simple? Figure 1.3 shows a blob, backlit, standing in a doorway.

Figure 1.4 represents something. Is it a well-designed character?

Figure 1.3 is not a character design. You have no expectations for the object, and it does not elicit much emotional response. Figure 1.4, though simple and only showing a shadow figure, nevertheless demands something from the viewer. You have expectations, whether right or wrong, about the character.

In today's high-tech environment, there should be no excuse for a bad character design as in the 1953 *Robot Monster* film. For the most part, we have the means and the budget to create good designs. Now it is up to us, the artists, to learn how to deliver a good design.

FIGURE 1.3   Is this a character design?

FIGURE 1.4   Is this more of a character design?

Along with the end goal of having a good design, we will always need to consider the practical issues of the character's design. The most visually appealing design in the world is worthless if it is not useful.

Character Design Issues and Limitations

So let's talk about some of the practical issues and limitations that are associated with a character's design. You must be aware of many issues as you work on a character design. Often, you will be able to sit down with the animators and modelers and get precise specifications for their needs. Other times, you will not have this contact and will need to know what general questions to ask so that the character will be correctly designed for its specific use or platform. Over time and with experience, you will gain general knowledge of what is expected and what the parameters are for a given platform. Not too long ago, a character of 1,000 polygons was very detailed for one of the current game platforms. If you didn't know this information (or didn't ask some of the correct questions about the limits of the platform you were working for), you, the modelers, and animators could either be in for a long and stressful project or it would be a very short relationship.

The following sections cover some issues and limitations that you as a character designer must be aware of before you start and as you work. The questions are only posed; solutions are not given on purpose because the questions and solutions will probably be different for each assignment.

How Will the Character Be Used?

You need to know if the character will appear as a supporting background object, a mid-ground prop, a foreground character, or the center of interest. A character that is closer to the camera generally needs more finesse and detail, but maybe not the same level of detail as a character at the same distance that is the center of focus. Human vision is very selective, and things on the periphery of our awareness will not need to be complicated.

How Will the Character Be Displayed?

Quite obviously, the needs associated with different media vary widely. A character in print will require much more detail than a character on the movie screen. A character for a movie will need more detail than a character on a video or television monitor. A TV or video character will need much more detail than a character in a handheld game.

How Close or Distant to the Camera Will the Character Be?

If the character will never be closer to the viewer than 100 meters, there's no need to add superfluous details that would be lost in the distance. The flip side is also true: if the character will be in close-up, make sure that you add convincing detail.

How Big or Small Is the Character Relative to Other Characters?

When designing for video games, the polygon count for a character is still an important issue. Larger characters may need more polygons. They may need much more detailed texture maps, too. A model of an insect character would be approached differently than one of an elephant.

Will the Character Be Animated?

A stationary character will have different needs than one that animates. For example, if the character will be standing stationary, then you will not need to be very concerned with how the joints would work. If your character will be animated, you must take much greater care when designing how things will bend and articulate.

How Many Angles Will the Character Be Viewed From?

If you are designing a character for print, you have only one viewing angle at a time. A side-scrolling game will have only one viewing angle at a time but may have multiple views used at different locations throughout the game. A movie or real-time 3D game character will need to be viewed from all angles.

How Much Movement Will the Character Have?

A character that will move only its arms, for example, may need more careful design than a stationary character. A completely mobile character will require a different design than a partially mobile one.

How Fast or Slow Will the Character Be Moving?

Don't assume that because a character moves, it will have to be more complicated and detailed than a stationary one. As the character's speed increases, you will reach a point of diminishing returns in terms of detail and geometry because a very fast-moving character may be viewed as mostly a blur and may need a very simple design.

Will the Character Be Close Enough to See Facial Expressions?

You will have to know if you need geometry to represent facial features or if a texture map will be enough in the final product. Obviously, if the character's expressions will be important to the role the character is to play, you must include additional detail in both the texture maps and in the geometry to be able to convey a convincing expression. While you, the character designer, will not be building the actual geometry or maybe not even working on the texture maps, it is important that you keep these issues in your mind.

Will the Character Need to Speak?

A character that speaks will have different geometry requirements than a silent one. A character that speaks will need a mouth that articulates and moves. This requires additional geometry in the model. The person that will be modeling the character will need a clear picture of what is expected and needed.

How Much Detail Will You Need in the Hands, Feet, Hoofs, Talons, Paws, Etc.?

There was a time in the not-too-distant past when hands were represented by blocks of geometry with painted texture maps. Characters that held items in their hands were often modeled with the item as an integral part of the hand. Now we are seeing characters with articulating appendages. You need to know if your character will be realistic, stylized, surreal, abstract, or something completely out of left field.

Will the Character Be Simple or Complex?

This depends completely on the end use. The only exception would be when your design may be much more detailed than the end use justifies because of potential multiple uses. An example is when the character that you are designing for a game will also be used in print advertising. While the game character would need to be somewhat simple, the print character could be more detailed and complicated.

Who Does the Character Need to Appeal to Visually?

Know your audience and design the character appropriately. The character you are designing for a target audience consisting of teenage boys would be entirely different than a character that is designed for toddlers or an elderly audience.

Can the Character Stand on Its Own Design If Taken out of Its Environment?

You need to check that your design would be understandable if you showed it to someone without any of the surrounding environment. For example, if you are designing a villain, could you take that villain, put it into another context, and still tell that the character is evil? If you could, then your design is working.

Is the Character's Silhouette or Profile Readable on Its Own?

A character with a strong and recognizable silhouette will be visually stronger, more understandable, and more appealing than one whose silhouette isn't. If your character is casting a shadow on a wall, does that shadow enhance the perception of the character? If it does, then the silhouette is enhancing the look of the design.

How Do You Simplify the Character Design to Work Within the Platform's Constraints?

Until recently, it was useless to design a game character with flowing clothing or hair. The game platforms simply couldn't render the character in real time, or the time and cost required to animate the cloth for pre-rendered characters was prohibitive. Simplifying a character design is not really that hard. The main thing to remember is to work from the general to the specific. If you need to simplify a great but very complicated character design, look for the most basic general shapes that make up the character. Use the basic shape that remains as the basis of your simplification process.

How Will the Character Animate?

If the character will animate, definitely make sure that you get some information from the animation department about what is needed and expected so your design will conform to the specifications.

Do You Really Need to Remember All of This?

Unfortunately, yes, you really are expected to remember all of these issues each time you design a character. Other issues will no doubt arise with each character-design project. These are critical parts of the process.

It is important that these questions be your constant and conscious companions as you design your characters. Eventually, they will become second nature, and you will not be aware that you are answering them as you design; rather, their influence will always show in the underlying structure of your designs.

CONCLUSION

In the next chapters, we will go beyond the practical and define a working method that is successful, and then we will begin to look at the magic in character design. We will specifically look at where successful ideas come from and what you can do to help yourself generate the most creative ideas possible.

2

DEVELOPING A
WORKING METHOD

This chapter is about the importance of developing a "working method," a series of steps you use to help organize the way you get a job done. You can benefit from defining a working method for every task that you may be asked to accomplish. Character design is no exception. If you are paddling a canoe without direction or method, you may end up paddling in a circle and never get anywhere. So it is with character design. If you randomly scribble and draw your ideas without direction, you will never get anywhere.

This chapter presents various ideas that will help you succeed when you are assigned a character design as a job or for your own enjoyment. These ideas are by no means the only way or necessarily the right way of doing things. This working method is simply one approach to achieving successful results. It is hoped that you will be able to take what you read and apply the method with your own vision and adjustments, or vary the methods to suit your own individual goals.

THE NEED FOR A METHODICAL AND SUCCESSFUL WAY OF WORKING

For some reason, artists tend to jump right into tasks where we are expected to draw and paint without having any sort of plan. This is because we love to sketch and draw so very much that everything else simply isn't worth worrying about. We sketch, draw, and often flounder around trying to come up with an idea. Occasionally we get lucky and come up with something useful. More often than not, we end up with an idea that may or may not be the best along with a trash can of dead ends.

There is a better way. Having a specific plan of how to approach the work will not only increase your productivity but will also lower your level of frustration. The following tasks, if you follow them in an orderly progression, will help you organize your thoughts and ideas. Then it will be easier to draw and paint a cohesive form as well as objectively gauge the success of your effort.

Identifying and Understanding the Problem

The first and most important thing to do when trying to solve any problem is to identify and understand the problem at hand. While that may sound obvious, most of us are sometimes guilty of rushing headfirst into the unknown ill prepared. Here we'll assume that your job is to design some sort of character. It does not matter who the character is for; if you don't clearly know what you're trying to accomplish, you will not be successful.

The first and sometimes hardest task to accomplish when you're identifying the problem is to make sure that both client and artist are visualizing the same thing. When a client and artist are discussing ideas, their different backgrounds can be a major obstacle to visually understanding what is needed in a character. Everyone perceives the world somewhat differently. Everything that we have experienced, been told, observed, or felt as children will affect how we view the world around us and, consequently, the images we create. If two people hear identical words or see identical images, they will not form mental images that are also identical. So it's very important to ensure that both parties understand exactly what the artist is being asked to do both visually and technically.

A typical scenario that an artist will face as a character designer might be the following:

1. The initial meeting between Sally, the artist, and Mr. Smith, the client, is going well, and both parties are excited about the scope of the project. The client tells Sally that he requires a great big, hairy, ugly villain who will pound the hero to a mushy pulp. He even uses hand gestures and sound effects to impress upon her the "badness" of the villain. Sally can see it now in her mind, and she has a clear picture of the direction that she will take with the character.
2. Once back at the studio, Sally starts drawing immediately, and the results are fantastic. This is quite possibly the finest sketch she has ever produced in such a limited amount of time, and she cannot wait to take it to Mr. Smith.
3. At the next meeting, she hands her sketch to the client with great expectation of being told that this is the finest villain ever drawn.
4. Mr. Smith's reaction is not what Sally expects; he casually tosses the sketch on the desk and tells her to try again. The rest of the meeting is a blur as she tries to figure out what happened and where she went wrong.

The problem in this scenario is that while the artist thought she understood the problem, in reality she did not clearly comprehend what was being asked of her. The client asked for several things. He wanted a villain that was big, ugly, and hairy. What did he mean when he said "big"? How many different interpretations can there be of the word "big"? What big means to one person may be entirely different than what it means to another.

When presented with such a description, an artist must find out exactly what is meant. For example, the character is big in relationship to what? The hero, an elephant, a mouse, or what exactly? The villain is big in what way? Is he tall? Muscular but not large in size? Fat or something else?

Can you see the problem? It's easy to see the same problem with the other descriptive words. What is meant by "ugly" and "hairy"? You can almost be certain that Sally's understanding is not the same as the client's.

So, how does an artist identify the problem so that everyone involved has the same understanding of what is being described? It is really very simple. Ask lots of questions. When you are told to make a character "big," respond with something like this: "You mean as big as an elephant?" Quite quickly, both you and the client will start to arrive at a shared vision.

When you have arrived back at your studio or desk, it is a very good idea to follow up the conversation with a written recap of the discussion. Write a memo or letter stating, "As per our discussion, this is what I understand you to be looking for in the character design." Be very specific in your memo. If the response is that yes, you understand exactly what is wanted, you're ready to go to the next step.

Analyzing the Problem and Breaking It Down into Simpler Elements

When you initially analyze the problem or end goal, you will look at the whole and start breaking it into manageable sections that are easily resolved. Most of these manageable sections are questions that you must answer before proceeding with the design phase.

Coming Up with Ideas to Solve the Problem

For the majority of artists, this is one of the best parts of the whole character-design process. The process of generating ideas is a combination of the visual, mental, and written. Without good ideas, you have nothing.

When you have solved all of the smaller problems, combine their solutions into larger ideas that all will solve the original problem. You should be able to come up with several different but acceptable solutions. The differences between the solutions may seem small and hardly significant, yet the more ideas you come up with, the greater your chance of hitting on a good idea.

Choosing the Best Idea

This is the tricky part. How do you tell what the best idea is? To a large degree, you will know simply by looking at your work. Some of your ideas will obviously be bad, and they will be easy to spot. After you have picked a few of the best, turn to a fresh eye so that you can narrow down the field of potential solutions. A coworker, friend, or even the art director will have a fresh perspective and should be able to give you good advice. Make sure that whomever you turn to will not patronize you and say how wonderful all of the ideas are; rather, you want that person to give you a true critique of how well the individual ideas have solved the problem.

Remember that the first idea is not usually the best; it is usually the most obvious one. Yet, if after much work, the first idea still seems to be the best, do not hesitate to go back to it.

Drawing the Character

This is the best part. Most artists find that there is nothing better than sitting down and drawing the day away. This is the reward for all of your hard preliminary work, and if you have successfully followed the first steps outlined earlier, you will know right where to go with the drawing.

Evaluating the Results

If all goes well, here is where you get the compliments and inflated ego. Your work will be loved, appreciated, and pivotal to the success of the project. If things do not go as well, don't be disheartened; sometimes the magic works, and sometimes it doesn't. This final evaluation of your work is often the hardest part.

Have no doubt that the client will evaluate if your character design succeeded and fits his needs . Do not be afraid of failure, and do not take failure personally. You will succeed and you will fail at various times and on various projects. If what you have done does not work, go back to step one and start again. As the old saying goes, "Success is 90 percent perspiration and 10 percent inspiration."

CONCLUSION

Trying to acquire good working habits from the very beginning of your career is very important to your long-term success. Use this suggested format or one of your own. Just make sure that all of the following steps appear somewhere in the process:

1. Identify precisely what the expectations for the character are. You must define the problem.
2. Analyze and simplify the defined problem into smaller, more manageable problems. Come up with ideas to solve your problems. When the small questions have been answered, combine the answers to solve the large problem.
3. Choose the best character ideas that you have developed.
4. Draw the character.
5. Look at your resulting drawings. Have others look at your results. Realistically evaluate what you have done.

If you follow these five steps (or some modification of their basic premises), you will almost be guaranteed success as you design your characters. In the next chapter, we will discuss specific ideas and methods for coming up with ideas for your characters or improving ideas that you may already have.

EXPANDING ON YOUR IDEAS WHEN CREATING THE CHARACTER

This chapter is about ideas—where they come from and how to develop the ones you have. There is no doubt that coming up with creative ideas is tough work. Nothing grows in a vacuum, and the best ideas and designs do not come easy. Artists often sit around in their studios or at their desks, virtually a vacuum, pondering where the next idea will come from. Often we sit and scribble on whatever paper is handy, tap the pencil, scribble some more, and then wonder where we lost our ability to think of good ideas.

Good character designs do not usually come from sitting, tapping a pencil, or jumping directly to the sketching. Planning and preliminary work are always needed and will pay great dividends in the finished design. This is what this chapter is all about. Here we present a few strategies to help charge your creative energy. These ideas are not the only things that you can do, but if you're stuck, they'll help get you rolling.

The majority of the exercises and suggestions presented in this chapter are about generating creative thought. While you need nothing more than your brain to give these ideas a try, you should probably have a pencil and paper ready in anticipation of that epiphany.

BASIC STRATEGIES TO HELP GENERATE CREATIVE IDEAS

Coming up with new and creative ideas for a character is, at best, a lot of work. It's harder to get inspired design ideas if you simply bounce them around in the confines of your mind. If possible, get all of your senses involved.

Learning to Relax

The first and most important thing you can do for yourself when you are faced with a creative problem is to take a deep breath and relax. Talk to yourself a little about the problem. Take another deep breath and make sure you are feeling calm and confident. The more you can lower your stress and anxiety levels, the better your chances for mental clarity will be as you begin coming up with ideas.

When you are calm, collected, and ready to start working on some great ideas, use a combination of the following suggestions to help you come up with creative ideas:

1. **Take a walk and clear your mind.** We're not talking a power walk, where you try to get exercise; we mean a stroll, during which you observe what is around you and your mind can wander. Daydream. Lie down on a grassy hill and look at the clouds. See the shapes within them and let the shapes you see suggest images to you. Sit down on a rock by a stream or river and watch the water. All of these things will help free your mind.
2. **Closely observe the people around you every day.** If you do this, you will begin to notice special qualities that you didn't see before. As your mind begins thinking about your basic character idea, consider applying to your character the individual qualities, traits, physical appearance, quirks, habits, and faults of your friends. Don't just limit yourself to friends. Include the larger circle of your acquaintances as well as celebrities, politicians, sports

stars, and anyone in the public eye. If you are designing a villain, why not base the character on people that you just do not like? You can also look at fictional characters, but watching them is not as much fun as observing real people. Remember that a fictional character is already someone else's vision and as such is nothing more than a shallow representation of a personality, whereas real people have much more depth.

3. **Have a brainstorming session with a few other people.** Brainstorming by yourself is never successful, but brainstorm with four or five people and see what happens. As an example of how well this works, try to think of 50 new and unique ways to use a brick. If you did this exercise alone, you probably couldn't come up with 50 variations, but if you get four or five creative people together in a room, they will likely come up with some very creative ideas. Of course, many of the ideas will not be usable. Usability is not the point, and it does not matter if some of the ideas are outrageous. The point is to begin looking at the subject in a new light. Figure 3.1 shows what it can sometimes feel like when you have to come up with new ideas.

FIGURE 3.1   Brainstorming can be painful but rewarding.

Locating Useful Reference Materials

Being able to find appropriate reference materials and learning how to use them is one of the most important abilities an artist can have. In fact, one of the most important skills you can acquire is knowing how to find information that will be useful and inspiring to you as you design your character. Learn how to use the local library. Learn how to use the Internet to find visually inspiring imagery; you can find anything on the Internet these days. The vast amount of visual and written information on the Web can be overwhelming if you are not careful, so make sure to spend your time effectively.

Using Wordplay

Playing with words can be one of the best ways to come up with good ideas. Basically, this exercise consists of writing columns of words and combining them in unusual ways. You can literally draw lines from one word to another. Combinations you never thought of will arise. If needed, take some time to create lists that are specific to the project you are working on. It would not do much good to list ocean creatures if you were working on a space character.

Here is an example of a very short list to illustrate the concept of combining words to form new ideas to work with. Of course, this list is not meant for any specific problem; the lists that you would use should be customized to your problem. Some combinations work better than others. A "sharp heroic" does not make much sense.

1. Knight
2. Obtuse
3. Shiny
4. Vicious
5. Mermaid
6. Heroic
7. King
8. Warthog
9. Sharp
10. Friendly
11. Monster
12. Ostrich

Fantasizing About the Character

Fantasize about the character that you need to design. Fantasizing goes hand in hand with both brainstorming and daydreaming. Fantasizing is more an individual activity where you would imagine "what if"-type situations about your character, whereas brainstorming is best in a group setting, as we have seen. When fantasizing, you will want to get out of the everyday modes of thought and see how far out you can take your ideas. "What if?" is the biggest question to ask yourself when you fantasize.

Using Symbolism with the Character

Give the character personality or traits that have symbolic elements. Many symbolic elements are very easy to relate to. If you use appropriate symbols, your audience will get quick clues to a character's personality. For example, if a halo is put over a character's head, assumptions can be made, whether right or wrong, about the character. The symbolism may be public and easily recognized by many people, or it may be private and have meaning only to you, the creator. Many books that list different symbols and their meanings are available. Some symbols are timeless, while others are more contemporary. Examples of some things with symbolic meaning are white doves, bats, black cats, gold, lead, the planets, and astrological symbols.

Building the Character Around a Myth

Build your character around a myth, or create a myth around your character. Mythologize your character. The human race has so many different myths and legends that it's easy—and to a degree smart—to use them as a basis for your characters because a mythical character's history is already so well defined. The character Dracula has become such a strong cultural symbol of the myth that designing a "new" Dracula would take a lot of work to break the visual mold.

Snowballing

Just as a snowball gains size and speed as it rolls down a hill, snowballing an idea can help it gain momentum and size. Snowballing is simply adding more and more wacky notions to a developing idea. Use snowballing in conjunction with brainstorming, fantasy, wordplay, or just about any other idea-creating exercise.

Visiting Special Places for Inspiration

Visit the zoo. Some of the best ideas can come when you watch the animals as well as the people. Figure 3.2 shows an unusual character based on someone seen at the zoo. Along these same lines, go and spend the day at the local airport with a sketchbook. You will be amazed by the amount of inspiration that walks by.

FIGURE 3.2   An interesting character seen at the local zoo.

DEVELOPING YOUR BASIC IDEA

Getting the basic idea of a character is always the hardest part of the creative process. By doing the simple things we discussed in the last section and not just sitting at your desk in the dark trying to be inspired, you will open up new avenues of experience that can lead to new ideas for your characters. However, the basic idea is only the first step. You now have a vision, but it is only a somewhat ghostlike visage on the edge of your conscience. Your basic idea is floating around either in your mind or on paper. You know where you want to go with this idea, but you're feeling somewhat lost as to a direction.

The strategies in the previous section are mostly cerebral, whereas the methods discussed here are best done visually with a piece of paper and pencil. Not only will you have a record of idea changes, but your drawings will also help generate additional ideas. Use relatively inexpensive paper and a soft pencil, marker, or pen.

Do not erase! This is very important. You are not drawing pretty pictures but generating differing ideas. An eraser will slow you down and kill the creative flow. No one else is meant to see the images you will create; they are just your thought processes and ideas coming to life. Don't expect them to look solid and refined at this point.

The following are some strategies to help you develop a basic but vague idea into a more concrete visual image ready to be drawn or sketched. They are not the only ways to firm up an idea but are good methods for continuing the process. As noted in the previous section, use these ideas in conjunction with each other.

Using Caricature

You can caricature just about anything you are drawing: people, animals, plants, and maybe even rocks. Caricature can be used to further develop ideas that seem to have gone stale. Quite often, caricature, while humorous, is looking for the essence of the subject. If you are having trouble seeing where to go with a design, try doing a caricature of what you already have. Once you have again found the essence of the caricature, continue with the design. Figure 3.3 shows an example of caricature.

FIGURE 3.3   A caricature of a family dog.

Using Humor

Humor is a great way to take an idea that is stalled and jump-start the creative process. Humor's main purpose is to entertain, and it generally does not need a lot of explanation. Humor does not try to make a statement. For example, if you are developing a serious barbarian character, put him in a humorous situation or change his props to something humorous (as in Figure 3.4) and see how many more creative vistas open for you.

FIGURE 3.4   A gladiator armed only with asparagus and a smile.

Using Blotter Pictures

So you are still stuck. You still need to design new and exciting characters and even costumes for them. Perhaps you should try using some blotter pictures to get some ideas brewing. Blotter pictures are the same thing as the famous Rorschach psychological test and are extremely easy to do on the computer. Figure 3.5 shows an example of a blotter picture.

FIGURE 3.5   A computer-generated inkblot.

Black and white as well as color work well. Black and white usually works better when you are trying to come up with ideas for form shapes (Figure 3.6), whereas
color tends to work better for ideas that are decorative in nature (Figure 3.7).

FIGURE 3.6   A black-and-white inkblot picture.

FIGURE 3.7   A color inkblot picture.

Using Exaggeration

Exaggeration, which is an integral part of caricature, is fairly self-explanatory. Take
your character idea and exaggerate some portion of it. The exaggeration can either be
extreme or subtle, depending on your intention. Be careful that you do not exaggerate everything within the character. After all, exaggeration is based on the difference

between things that we consider the norm and things that are not the norm. Figure 3.8 shows an already exaggerated face that has been exaggerated even more.

FIGURE 3.8   An exaggerated character.

Using Satire

Satire is humor but with teeth. The teeth can be large and very sharp, or small and relatively painless. Humor becomes satire when it begins to deliver a message. The humor in satire is almost always aggressive and critical with the purpose of entertaining or scolding while delivering its message. Political cartoonists are experts at using satire with a character.

Using Parody

Parody is one step beyond satire and needs the viewer's knowledge of the subject to work. Parody can simply entertain like humor, try to educate or scold like satire, or try to do both. For the parody to work, the audience must be familiar with the original subject and be able to see the similarities between both the original and the changed version. For example, a fat little Dracula-type character dressed in white would be a parody of the classic version we are all familiar with.

Doing Some Expression Exercises

So every character that you draw has the facial expression of a zombie. No wonder the characters lack life. Every character needs to have expression, and the majority of that expression is found in the face and body language. A good way to practice drawing facial expressions is to revert to the most basic elements that drive an expression:

the eyes, nose, and mouth. As quickly as possible, draw a series of expressions using only lines for the facial features. Some of them will be garbage, but some will look like something. Take the ones that look like something and develop them further.

Doing Some Five-Dot Action Exercises

Similar to expression exercises, five-dot action exercises help the artist get out of the doldrums of static character poses. The exercise is simple to set up but harder to complete. Take a dozen or so pieces of paper and have a coworker draw five dots on each. Each page of dots should be different. It really does not matter if the dots are in some sort of order or completely random. When you have the paper back, draw your character on each page using four of the dots to represent each individual hand and foot; the fifth dot will represent the head. If your character is not a quadruped, include additional dots as required.

Using Folded Paper

This exercise usually allows you to come up with some very interesting results. Three or four artists each draw a section of a character on a folded piece of paper. No artist can see the previous artist's work, save for the lower eighth of an inch or so of the previous drawing. Taking that small section and knowing what part of the character the artist is expected to draw, each artist completes the assigned section, folds the page so that only the bottom bit is showing, and passes it to the next artist. Several iterations of this exercise can often lead to extraordinary images and ideas.

Using Idealization

The concept is as simple as it sounds. Take your character idea and make it the ideal of whatever it is. Knowing what the ideal of a character is makes it easier to make a realistically flawed character.

Adding and Subtracting

Just like in math, you can add and subtract parts of the character. First, you can try adding things to the design, such as actual body parts, a costume, or some equipment. Then, do the reverse. Take your character and begin removing things—body parts or accessories; it does not matter. The method is simply to get you to look at things differently.

Using Repetition

Somewhat similar to the technique of adding and subtracting is using repetition. Take an element of the design and repeat it numerous times. Once again, do not be limited by your imagination; rather, let your imagination run wild.

Using Combinations

Combining differing elements has always been one of the sparks that fires an artist's imagination. Who would have thought to combine a horse with a human? Combine any number of differing elements and see what is possible. This strategy is similar to the wordplay method we discussed earlier in this chapter in that you are combining ideas. If it helps, write down the different things that you are considering combining and make choices from the list. Combine organic and inorganic elements. Combine geometric and organic shapes.

Transferring Characteristics

Try transferring the characteristics from one object to another. This is a simple concept. Transfer characteristics from an inorganic object to an organic one. Or try transferring the characteristics from something mechanical to a plant. Transferring characteristics is about transferring the physical as well as the not-so-physical attributes between objects and characters.

Superimposing

Superimposing is similar to combining characters or objects, except that instead of mixing two separate objects together, you are superimposing one over the other. This can be done at more than one level. Again, you are encouraged to try things that you normally would not consider doing.

Changing the Scale

Take a part of your idea and change the scale. Change the scale of your whole character if it will work. To effectively change the scale of an object, you must include something within the image or on the character to give a visual clue as to the scale. Making a character a giant does not work unless something around the character gives visual clues to the imposing size. The reverse is also true if you are making a diminutive character.

Substituting

Substitute a portion or prop of your character with something different. Perhaps even substitute something really different. Make that sword a paintbrush or vice versa.

Distorting

Distortion is very self-explanatory. Shear, twist, fold, spindle, and mutilate your character, portions of your character, the original idea, the costume, anything. Nothing is sacred or beyond your ability to distort.

Disguising the Character

Change the appearance of your character with disguise. Possibly all you need to add is something as simple as sunglasses. Or maybe sometimes you need something more extreme, such as sunglasses with a fake nose and a mustache.

Using Analogy

Take two of your character designs and create an analogy between them. Take different characters and make something about them similar. For example, how could you make a weight lifter and ballerina seem more similar? Could you add a tutu to the weight lifter? Could you add something else? As you see what the results are, continue with differing and additional characters.

Creating a Hybrid

Create a hybrid by taking two of your characters and imagining that they produce offspring. What would happen if one of the characters were a robot and the other were a plant? No combination is too outrageous.

Evolving the Character

Evolution is a very subtle process, with change being gradual and sometimes hardly visible. Evolving a character can be one of the most fun and rewarding ways of creating new and exciting characters. Simply pick something about your character design and modify it slightly. Take this changed character and then alter the changed element slightly. Continue with this type of progression as long as you like.

Changing the Character with Metamorphosis and Mutation

The opposite of evolving a character is to metamorphose or mutate that character. Metamorphoses and mutations are dramatic changes. A common example of a metamorphosis would be how a caterpillar changes into a butterfly. Metamorphoses are generally caused by some internal action. On the other hand, the dramatic changes that are the result of a mutation are generally caused by an outside influence. Taking your character design and metamorphosing or mutating it into a different character is risky. There is a good chance that you will lose the original idea if you're not careful.

Using Metaphors

A metaphor is a figure of speech where a word or phrase that usually means one thing is used to describe another; in a sense, you are comparing the two things. You can use this to great advantage when designing similar yet different characters.

Using Visual Puns

A pun is when you play with similar-sounding words that have different meanings, or different-meaning words with the same sound. The visual equivalent of a pun can be a good way of generating new and creative ideas. Good sources for visual puns are cliché sayings.

Doodling and Scribbling

Simply sitting down and beginning to scribble and doodle is a great way to expand on an idea that is just forming. Doodles and scribbles should be quickly executed with little detail until the idea begins to solidify.

Making Things Look Strange, or Transforming the Ordinary into the Fantastic

As you develop your character idea, take some of the idea and see how strange you can make the figure look while still being recognizable. This technique works very well for a character's props and costumes. In general, the more you can push an idea, the better the ideas you come up with will be.

Using Mimicry

Mimicry is a technique of deception that is very common in the animal world. Many harmless creatures take on the physical attributes of other, more dangerous creatures. This has the direct benefit of scaring off predators. This is the opposite of camouflage, as the mimic generally wants to be noticeable and advertise its deceptive danger. Though this is not generally a good method of character design because of the tendency to confuse the audience, it is nevertheless a great way of generating new ideas.

CONCLUSION

Chapter 2 suggested some activities that could help you begin to formulate ideas when presented with the challenge of designing characters. This chapter described a number of rather specific ideas that can help you expand on a very basic idea you've already developed. From here on in, the book will assume that you now have a pretty solid idea of where your character design is headed. The next chapters will help you create the finished products. First, we will start by creating the character's history. From there, we will explore the personality and physical look of the character.

MAKING THE CHARACTER REAL BY CREATING A CHARACTER HISTORY

Chapters 1 through 3 were about coming up with ideas. This chapter expands on your ideas so you can actually design the character's look. By now you should have some basic ideas about your character and possibly a few sketches. The image of your character is becoming clearer, and, for the most part, you are feeling pretty good about your design. Now is the time to think about the history and look of the character.

This chapter is about making your character real and about communicating aspects of the character to others. Doing so allows you to help the modelers and animators see the character as real as possible. It will also help you, the designer, put the finishing touches on your character.

CREATING THE CHARACTER'S HISTORY

You may be wondering what the point of having a character history is. The character you are designing is only for a video game, after all, and not an epic novel. Well, a character history helps you, the designer, truly get to know what you are going to be drawing. Having a history for your character helps you pose the small questions that will give you the insight needed to make a successful design.

The steps to creating a character's history are simple and involve no more than answering a few questions. Be sure to write the history down as either a list or simple, descriptive paragraphs.

The next few sections cover the things you should consider when thinking about what your character's history will be.

The Character's Past, Present, and Future

Just as your friends and acquaintances are much more interesting when you know something about them, your character will be more interesting to the audience when something more is known about it. Consider the following about your character:

The character's past. Where is your character from, and what were the character's formative years or youth like? Has the character had a very mobile past, or was the character born and raised in one area? Your character may not always have a distant past; maybe your character is only a week old and the past is not an issue.

The character's present situation. What has been happening with and to your character within the past few days, weeks, or months? Where is the character currently living and why?

The character's future. Isn't it wonderful that you are psychic and can see the future of your character? Use this information to help you develop the character's present.

The Character's Everyday Environment

The question of environment is an important one. Quite often, the environment that a character lives in will to a large degree determine the general physical look of your creation. Consider the following:

- Where is the character from? What specific environment did your character originate in?
- Where does the character live now?
  - Outer space? Will the character need a space suit to operate in our typical earth environment?
  - Aquatic? Will the character be slimy and breathe through gills?
  - Subterranean? Will the character have large digging claws and no eyes?
  - Airborne? Will the character be light as a feather or winged?
  - Surface dweller? Will the character resemble a human?
  - Some exotic environment? Will the character be a methane breather that drinks ammonia?
  - A combination? Will the character be some combination of the above?

Considering where your character is from will help you arrive at a general physical look very quickly. From that point, you can experiment to your heart's desire as far as the small touches.

The Character's Personality

If you answer the following questions, you will begin to get a good feel of what a character's personality will be based on. Once you have the reasons for the way a character should behave, you can then figure out how that character will actually act. Here are the questions to ask:

- What is your character's personality and how has your character's history affected that personality?
- What is the character's name? This sounds obvious, but you would be surprised how many characters don't have a name.
- What is the character's family tree?
- Is the character based on legend or myth? If the character is based on one, will the audience know and understand the origin of the legend or myth?
- Is the character based on another's work? If so, is the author living or deceased? Will you have any licensing issues if the character is too recognizable?
- Was the character born, created, or hatched?
- What is the character's body language, and how does that help define the personality? Subconsciously, we all read each other's body language. Make sure that your character's body language fits the character's personality, profession, or gender.

- Was the character's family life good, bad, neutral, or nonexistent?
- Is the character educated or illiterate? An educated caveman will behave entirely different than an uneducated caveman. Likewise, an educated caveman will be different than an educated astronaut. Make sure the education is appropriate to the character.
- What are the character's current living conditions? Is the character obsessively or compulsively neat, or is slob a more apt description? Are the character's living conditions advanced or primitive?
- Does the character have a job, trade, or commercial skill? Though this may not directly affect the look or feel of a character, it may. A lumberjack assassin will look different than a ballet dancer assassin.
- Does the character need a commercial skill? Again, this may or may not affect your character design.
- Does the character have or need a financial status? A rich character may be able to outfit itself better than a poor one. A rich character will possibly be able to hire others to do his bidding.
- What are the character's favorite foods?
- Does the character have any favorite activities, hobbies, etc.?

The Character's Personality Traits

It is so very important to get to know your character. If you answer these simple questions when you are laying the foundation for your design, your design will be believable and living to the audience:

- Is the character slow to anger or constantly in a rage?
- Is the character shy or bold?
- Is the character greedy or generous?
- Is the character sneaky or gullible?
- Is the character superstitious?
- How romantic is the character?
- Does the character have any personality quirks such as twitches, psychoses, or phobias?
- What, if any, are the character's defining moments?
- Has the character had any triumphs or failures?
- How does the character treat others?
- What are the character's politics?
- Is the character religious?
- Does the character own property?
- Does the character have servants, pets, a harem, etc.?
- Does the character have any unusual mental or physical characteristics?
- What are the character's day-to-day activities?
- Is your character a couch potato or a soldier?

The Character's Look

Once you know your character's personality, it is just as important to know his or her look. Ask yourself the following questions to help refine your mental image of the character:

- How technically advanced is the character? Is he a caveman, space jockey, or bottom-dwelling scum sucker?
- What are the character's defensive capabilities?
- What are the character's offensive capabilities?
- Does the character wear clothing, armor, or costumes?
- Does the character have style, and, if so, what is that style like?
- What are the audience's expectations for the character? What does the audience expect visually? How does the audience expect the character to act?

CONCLUSION

If you can answer all the questions mentioned in this chapter, you will "know" your creation, which is vital to a good design. In the next chapter, you'll learn some basic questions to ask yourself so that you can finalize the physical look of the character.

5

DESIGNING THE PHYSICAL LOOK OF YOUR CHARACTER

This chapter gives you some questions to ask yourself as you are refining your mental image of the character. For the most part, you can use this chapter as an outline of things to consider when you begin drawing the character. For these exercises, you just need some paper and a few sharp pencils.

DESCRIBING THE CHARACTER

So what does your character look like? By this time, you probably have a vague mental image of what your character will look like, but can you describe the look to the audience? This section will help you develop that mental image into a specific look for your character.

The Character's General Physical Characteristics

Here are some general aspects of the character to consider:

- What is the character's general physiology and body makeup?
- If the character has legs, how many are there? Is your character a biped or a quadruped, or does the character have more than four legs?
- Is your character animal-like? What kind of animal does it resemble? Is it like a mammal, bird, reptile, amphibian, fish, insect, some lower form of life, or something else entirely that is alive only in your mind?
- How many appendages besides legs does the character have?
- How many heads are there? Does one dominate, or do all of them think and react alike?
- How many arms are there, and where are they positioned?
- Does your character have wings? If so, what kind? Are they like those of a bat, bird, or insect? Are they fin-like?
- Does your character have a tail? Does it have more than one, and where are the tails located?
- Is anything extra attached to the character?
- How and what does the character eat? Is the character a carnivore and kind of scary, or a mild-mannered and gentle herbivore? Is the character an omnivore or insectivore?

The Character's Body Type

You need to decide if the character will have one of the three kinds of body types, or if the character is something else entirely. The three body types are as follows:

Ectomorph. Those with this body type have the following characteristics:
- Are thin
- Have small bones

- Have a flat chest
- Are delicately built
- Are young and youthful in appearance
- Are tall
- Are lightly muscled
- Have stooped shoulders
- Have a large brain
- Have difficulty gaining weight
- Take longer to grow muscles
- Have a short upper body
- Have long arms and legs
- Have long and narrow feet and hands
- Have very little body fat
- Have a narrow chest and narrow shoulders as well as long, thin muscles
- Have a high metabolism

Endomorph. Those with this body type have the following characteristics:
- Have a soft body
- Have large bones
- Have a slow metabolism
- Have underdeveloped muscles as well as a small amount of muscle mass and small muscles
- Have a round-shaped body
- Have an overdeveloped digestive system
- Have trouble losing weight
- Generally find it easy to build muscle
- Have short musculature
- Have a round face
- Have a short neck
- Have wide hips
- Have a high body fat percentage

Mesomorph. Those with this body type have the following characteristics:
- Have a hard, muscular body
- Have medium-sized to large bones
- Have a medium to high metabolism
- Have an overly mature appearance
- Have a rectangular-shaped body
- Have thick skin
- Have a low to medium body fat percentage
- Have a large amount of muscle mass and large muscles
- Have an upright posture
- Gain or lose weight easily
- Grow muscle quickly

- Have a large chest
- Have a long torso
- Are very strong

Within the body types, there are other things to consider, such as the body style. Is the character fat, skinny, buff, or a combination of different body styles?

The Character's Proportions

Here are some things to consider about the character's proportions:

- Is the character built like a superhero, an ordinary guy, or a 98-pound weakling?
- How does the environment affect the character's proportions? A character from a high-gravity environment, for example, will be very different from a character from a low-gravity environment. You also need to think about the effect of temperature extremes on the character's proportions.

The Character's Makeup

You need to consider what the character is made of. Your character could be made of any of the following or a combination thereof:

- Flesh and bones
- Plants
- Metal
- Plastic
- Stones or minerals

Or perhaps the character is ethereal, like a ghost or a flame.

The Character's Gender

There are various characteristics to consider here:

- Is the character male, female, a hermaphrodite, or something else entirely?
- What are the primary physical differences of the genders?
- What are the secondary physical differences of the genders?

The Character's Surface

You need to consider the following about the character's surface covering:

- Does the character have skin? If so, what are the color, texture, and hairiness, and are there variations from body part to body part?
- Does the character have fur? If so, what are the color, texture, and thickness, and are there variations from body part to body part? If the character has fur, does the character shed?

- Does the character have scales? If so, what are the color, texture, and thickness, and are there variations from body part to body part?
- Does the character have feathers? If so, what are the color, texture, and thickness, and are there variations from body part to body part?
- Does the character have a shell, slime, cilia, or something else entirely?

The Character's Color

What range of colors is the character? How does the character's color affect the audience's perception of the character? Is the character able to change colors like a chameleon? Are differing parts of the character different colors? Are the character's colors used for camouflage or warning?

The Character's Facial Structure

You need to consider the following regarding the character's face:

- What is your character's facial structure, and what are the character's facial features?
- How many faces and features are there?
- How many eyes are there? How expressive are the character's eyes?
- Does the character have breathing parts or some other breathing structure?
- Does the character have mouth parts?
- Will the character be capable of speech?
- Does the character have antennae or something else entirely?
- Where are the features placed in relation to each other?

The Character's Movement

Here are some things to consider as far as how the character moves:

- What is the character's method of motion? Does the character fly, swim, crawl, burrow, walk upright or on all fours, squirm, or hop? Is it jet propelled like an octopus, or does it travel around on wheels?
- How does your character move when in motion?
- When the character begins to move, which body part moves first, and which moves last?
- How does the character carry its weight when in motion, and how does the character stand?
- How does the character move when idle or when nervous? What about when angry or frightened?
- Is there a particular stance or pose that defines the character's attitude about life?

Other Considerations

If you answer the questions posed throughout this chapter, you will have a pretty concrete idea of what your character looks like. Here are a few miscellaneous but important things to keep in mind when designing a character:

Using stereotypes. To add a degree of familiarity to your character, you can carefully use stereotypes when appropriate and not offensive. After all, we do typically associate certain characteristics with different character types. Barbarians, for example, are not generally skinny 98-pound weaklings.

Fooling the audience. Don't try to do this. Make bad guys look like bad guys. Make the monsters threatening, for example. The audience expects a certain personality for different looks. Do not stray too far from the expected, or you will confuse the audience.

Being sensitive. Always remember to be sensitive and careful when you are dealing with and using cultural and symbolic elements in your creations.

Providing scale. Remember to give a clue as to the scale of your character. If you create a giant, you must place something near him to give a sense of scale. Without anything to identify the scale of a character, the audience will have no idea of its size. The same character could be perceived as a giant or a midget depending on how you outfit your character and its surroundings.

Connecting the character to reality. Make sure there is some connection to reality. Your character needs to have a point of reference. If you create something that is unrecognizable, your audience will not relate to the character. It is no accident that most monsters walk and act generally like we do. We recognize the look of creatures that resemble ourselves and have expectations for how a character will generally behave.

Being original. Try to balance between using kitsch and being totally original. Kitsch is something that appeals to popular or lowbrow taste and is often of poor quality. Use kitsch items sparingly when designing your character. Kitsch can add a subtle sense of humor, but if it's overdone, it will look silly. Unless you have a good reason, generally try to avoid fads. They will date the character immediately. Not much is truly original anymore, but do make it a point not to blatantly copy another's works and ideas.

The Visual Issues of Character Design and How to Communicate Your Ideas

One of the easiest ways to communicate your character ideas is by using comparison. If the character is soft and delicate, make the character round without many angles. If the character is rough and ready, the design should be made of angular shapes.

Here are some other tips:

Working from the general to the specific. Doing this when designing is always well founded. If your character is understandable early on, the greater are the chances of him being understandable as you move along with your design.

Simplify when possible. As in just about everything in life, the simplest statements are generally the easiest to understand. You have no idea how sophisticated your audience may be, but aim for a simple design that will work with all levels of understanding

Do not use too many little bits and pieces. You will only confuse your audience. Remember that the devil is in the details. Don't overdo it. You recognize your friends by their general look and not by how many freckles they have on their nose.

Build characters out of basic shapes. Just about everything we see in the world around us can be built out of a few basic shapes: cubes, spheres, cones, and cylinders. Try to base your character on these basic shapes.

Test the silhouettes of your character. If the silhouette visually stands on its own, the character design will be stronger.

Maintain consistency in the character's environment. Variety is the spice of life, but when you are designing characters for the same environment, they should have a similar look and feel.

Avoid repeating the same formula over and over again when designing. For example, do not put a beard on every character.

CONCLUSION

Remember that being able to communicate your ideas through your character is one of the most important things that you can do as a character designer. Your character serves dual purposes, and it must fill each equally well. First are the needs of the media for which you are designing it; second, you must fulfill your own creative needs. Following the ideas presented in this and previous chapters will help you accomplish each of these goals. In the next chapter, we will take the idea you have developed and begin to explore some of the more traditional artistic principles that will help you communicate this idea effectively to your audience.

ARTISTIC PRINCIPLES FOR A DIGITAL AGE

Why would a book that is dedicated to digital art contain a part on traditional artistic principles? While the argument can be made that judging art is a subjective business, there is no argument that all good art is based on very nonsubjective principles.

In today's fast-paced, information-overloaded digital age, we sometimes overlook the very basic principles and strategies that the craft of art is based on. The computer is such a powerful tool, and the software that we use anticipates our needs so well that there is a tendency to let the technology do all of the work. This is why there is such a big market in program plug-ins. Click a button, and, all of a sudden, the image looks like a painting. This approach of letting the computer make the decisions is simply wrong and shortsighted if your goal is to create true digital art. It may also be the reason that there is so much hesitancy for the public to accept digital works as art, because of the perception that the computer has done the work.

This is why a part of this book is dedicated to traditional principles. If you are a beginner, you may not have ever had a discussion on value and color or their uses. If you are a professional, maybe you are letting the ghost in the machine do a little too much of the work. Either way, a refresher on traditional picture-making principles is appropriate in a book on digital painting.

Go through this part and read each chapter. Then, in your next image, try to use some of the information in your painting. Your work should definitely improve.

BASIC PRINCIPLES FOR IMPROVING THE DRAWING, SKETCHING, AND PAINTING OF YOUR CHARACTER

This chapter presents you with a few tips to help you with your figure and character work. Some of these things will sound obvious, and you have probably heard many of them before; however, some may be new to you. Your work will improve if you do them.

SOME BASIC IDEAS ABOUT DRAWING

If you remember these simple ideas as you are drawing, you will notice a dramatic, positive change in the quality of your sketches:

The first thing you can do to improve your figure work is to draw constantly. This should sound obvious, yet most of us become comfortable with a level of competence that is far below our capabilities. Though it's good to draw anything, concentrate on the figure. You need to focus on the figure because artists know intimately what the figure looks like and we should be able to easily spot our problems when drawing it. Drawing a tree is fine, but you can move a branch up or down six inches and no one will ever care. Move an arm up or down six inches, and it's guaranteed that everyone will notice. Practice drawings should be concerned with accuracy and do not have to be beautiful.

Draw from the living figure if possible. Drawing from a living figure is the only way to learn to impart a sense of life in one's work. When working from life, you learn how to adapt to the small changes that you see, as the model invariably shifts and moves slightly. If drawing from life is not feasible, draw the figure from available pictures.

When you begin a drawing, lightly place spots on the paper that will help define the outermost points of the figure. Place a mark on your paper that corresponds with each spot of the body that extends farthest from the body's center point. These marks, if connected, will form an envelope that will encompass the entire figure and will give you a framework within which you can work.

Always start with the general and work toward the specific. Start by drawing the simplest shapes that you see. Make them exactly correct and then start adding the smaller shapes. If you get the big picture right, the little picture can do nothing but follow.

Avoid drawing the eyelashes. Actually, avoid drawing any of the small details that really add nothing to the character and the essence of your drawing. The devil is in the details. You can recognize someone you know at a great distance not by seeing the color of her eyes but by the essence of her being. This is what you want to strive for in your work—the accurate representation of the essence of the figure.

Make your proportions correct. Surprisingly, many pieces of figurative art have awful proportions. With all the available information in books, there is no excuse for not learning it. By knowing what an average human looks like, you will have a greater chance for success when distorting the figure to fill your specific needs.

Learn your surface anatomy. Knowing how the muscles play out on the surface of the figure makes sketching and building models much easier with more believable results. Learning this information will also help you design nonhuman characters better.

Some Basic Ideas About Painting Figures, Hair, and Flesh Tones

Now we'll switch from drawing to painting. This section covers a few things for you to remember as you strive to do your best painting on your character work.

One of the most confusing aspects of painting a character is how to paint good flesh tones. Let's learn some of the secrets of painting good flesh tones.

A certain young art student wanted to know the "secret" formula for painting good flesh tones. He of course tried all the available tube mixtures, but he generally got awful results. This student finally thought he had found the secret one day when he stumbled on the oil color burnt sienna. What a great color. Burnt sienna can be mixed with white and will give you this beautiful, peachy flesh color. Unfortunately, using this color led to unexpected results. The paintings had a boring and unrealistic feel to them. The student had not yet found the secret formula, because there is no secret formula.

The following are some hints and tips to help you "paint" your characters better:

There are no secret formulas for flesh colors. Flesh color varies greatly from person to person and from different locations on the body. In traditional painting, all your flesh colors can be mixed with a red, yellow, and cool color (blue, green, black, etc.). Though you don't mix colors digitally the same way, the reasoning would be the same; you should use cooled-down pinks, oranges, and yellows.

Generally speaking, make the flesh tones of your male characters darker than those of your female characters. In most ethnic ranges, you can almost always get away with slightly lighter skin for your female characters.

The general complexion for a figure is found in the chest area. As you move out along the figure, the flesh tones become ruddier and darker. The hands, feet, elbows, and knees are distinctly redder and darker in appearance than the skin color in the center of the chest.

The face can be divided into three zones of color. From the hair line to the eyebrows is a zone of golden color. From the eyebrows to the bottom of the nose is a zone of red color. From the bottom of the nose to the bottom of the chin is a zone of blue or cooler color. These zones of colors should be played up much more in male characters than in female ones. Figure 6.1 shows these three zones.

FIGURE 6.1   The zones of color in the face.

Look for highlights. You can find them in the following locations: the bridge and tip of the nose, the corners of the eyes, the corner where the nostrils meet the face, the upper lip, the corners of the mouth, and the chin. Highlights are almost always in these spots, with slight variations. They can act like signs on a map to help you make sure that your features are properly located. Figure 6.2 shows highlighting on the face.

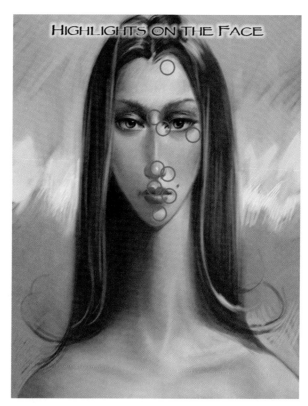

FIGURE 6.2   The location of highlights on the face.

Skin acts very much like a white surface in its interaction with the surrounding environment. Skin will reflect and be affected by colors from everything around it. A figure in a red costume will have much redder skin than a figure in a blue costume.

Here are some other things to keep in mind when you are drawing a face:

- Skin almost always reflects back into itself with an orange hue.
- Make sure that you always put some of the background colors into your skin tones.
- Make sure that there is a full range of value from lights to darks within your flesh tones. (This has nothing to do with ethnic backgrounds, as you will find lights in darker-skinned people and darks in lighter-skinned individuals.)
- Dark-skinned people have shinier skin than light-skinned people do.
- The highlights on the skin always have a tint of the light's color in them.
- Fleshy areas tend to be warm, while bony areas will be cooler.

- Dark skin has more blue in it than light skin. Dark skin that has been exposed to the sun has more reddish tones than blue ones.
- Ruddy-toned skin has a lot of violet touches.
- Mid-tone skin has a lot of golden colors.
- Light skin is usually very cool.
- Stay away from using too much yellow when painting blond hair. Use lots of warm, yellowish grays and cooled brown with touches of yellow in the highlights.
- Red hair has lots of oranges and purples in the light areas.
- The highlights on black hair often appear bluish. The same is true for dark brown hair but not to the same degree.
- Use deep red colors to draw the lines between lips and nostrils, lines between fingers, etc. Using a dark brown or black will kill the feeling of life in the art.
- Keep your colors in the flesh cooler than you think you need to.

The Art Part: Sketching, Drawing, and Painting the Character

When you are in the sketch phase, your ideas really come to life. There are also a number of other very good reasons to develop your ideas in quick sketches:

- Sketches are quick and inexpensive. Pencils and paper are relatively cheap.
- You can revise and rework your ideas quickly.
- You can quickly progress from very basic ideas to very detailed depictions of your character.
- You can get almost immediate feedback. When you look at sketch designs, it is very easy for the client to say whether things are going in the right direction.

Depending on your mood, sketch directly on the computer or just on paper. Either way is fine.

It is usually a good idea to sketch your character from several angles and possibly with several expressions. This approach may help you catch problems with your look and feel.

Here are some things you must know and remember to do so that the character will be pleasing both to you and the audience:

- You must know what the things you are drawing look like. Therefore, the following is very important:
  - You must know anatomy, both human and animal.
  - You must know about balance and how to make sure that your character has it.
  - You need to be aware of figure composition, or how to display the figure in a pleasing arrangement with its surroundings.
  - You need to be able to draw with both a simplicity and intensity in your work. You need simplicity so that the viewer can see the idea first; you need intensity so that the viewer can see the emotion and mood in your picture.

- You need to be able to combine your character with props and objects in an intelligent and visually pleasing fashion. The right props make your character designs effective. Bad props make for bad pictures.
- You must be able to express rhythm and motion in your character drawings. Rhythm is not the depiction of excessive action but the implied motion of the figure. Movement refers to actual depiction of motion within your drawing.
- You must be able to place emphasis where you want, and control the center of interest and the focal point of your images.

CONCLUSION

This chapter has presented some ideas on how to make drawings and paintings of your characters easier and better looking. While these ideas are not really profound in and of themselves, as a whole they often will make a difference between a bad-to-average drawing and a good-to-excellent one. It is good practice to review these ideas periodically so that they will eventually become second nature to you. In the next chapter, we will discuss value and its use in your art. For some reason, value is an easy subject to understand, but it is hard to implement in many artists' work. It is hoped that the next chapter will give some insight into this elusive subject.

VALUE AND ITS USE IN PICTURE MAKING

This chapter is about the most important artistic principle in picture making: value. Nothing is more important than value when you are making 2D images, especially if you are creating representational art. When you get the values correct in your images, you can do whatever you would like with the color, and the picture will still work visually. If your values are wrong, no amount of color will overcome the problems associated with placing the values in the wrong place.

Value is why we can see the world around us and then interpret that world onto a 2D surface. Look at Figure 7.1. What is the picture of?

FIGURE 7.1 A polar bear in a blizzard.

Isn't it obvious that it's a polar bear at the North Pole during a blizzard? This figure illustrates that without the value differences, we could not see the world around us. You can prove this to yourself. Simply close the door and turn off the light in a room with no windows. Your ability to see the world around you—let alone draw that world—is dramatically crippled. Many of us have visited a cave where the guide turned out the light. You cannot see a thing because there is absolutely no value difference in the space surrounding you.

We are so dependent on value to perceive the world around us that we really do not need color at all to visually understand our environment. Black and white imagery works so well that we can often accept it as a representation of reality without any color. This is best demonstrated by the success of black and white photography.

Now that you are convinced that value is the most important principle when you are creating either traditional or digital art, let's go over a few principles that may help you use value wisely when creating your art. If you are interested in trying out the information presented here on your own, you can use just about any 2D application.

What Is Value?

Value is the relationship of one part or detail in an image to another part of the image with respect to either the lightness or darkness of those parts and details.

Often, we get so caught up in color we forget that without value, there would be no color. A piece of art with the correct values in the right places will be understandable even if the color is wrong. The reverse is not necessarily true. Occasionally when working on your art, convert your piece to a grayscale image. Does it still hold up visually? If you are being too influenced by color, you will quite clearly see problem areas caused by the lack of value patterns.

Most of us already know what value is. The problem comes in knowing what to do with it. The careful use of value can help you create dramatic, meaningful, and easily understood visual images. Misuse of values will lead to the viewer's visual fragmentation and confusion.

The principles of using value are the same for traditional art and computer art. In either medium, value can do three things for you, the artist, either individually or in combination: the description of objects, the expressive, and the decorative.

The most common use of value is the description of objects. We see the world around us because of the patterns and shapes created on and by objects when light falls on them. These patterns and shapes are simply the light and shadows that we see. Figure 7.2 shows a group of simple objects that are seen because of their value differences.

There are only two kinds of shadows: form shadows and cast shadows. Form shadows are the most useful for the artist because they describe the light and dark sides of objects. Everything we see has parts that either face the light or not. The transition from the light to dark can be gradual on curving surfaces or abrupt on angular surfaces. In general, the more gradual the turn of a form, the softer the shadow will be. Cast shadows are pretty easy to understand. If something gets between an object and the light source, it will cast a shadow. Figure 7.3 shows both cast and form shadows.

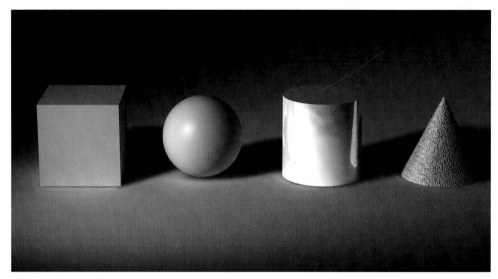

FIGURE 7.2   Objects in the world are seen because of value.

FIGURE 7.3   Cast and form shadows.

Each shadow gives us the visual cues we need to recognize what we are looking at. The dividing line between the light and dark sides of an object can give a good indication as to how far the object is from the light. The more shadow there is, the closer the light source is, as shown in Figure 7.4.

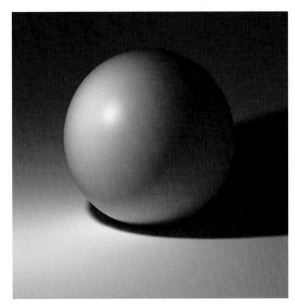

FIGURE 7.4   The light source is close to the object.

Likewise, the less shadow there is, the farther away the light source is, as shown in Figure 7.5.

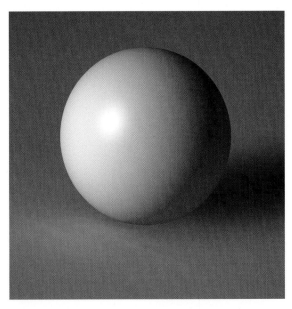

FIGURE 7.5   The light source is distant from the object.

Cast shadows tend to be very crisp and sharp when close to the object, gradually softening as they stretch out, as shown in Figure 7.6.

FIGURE 7.6   A cast shadow.

The size and shape of the shadow depends on a number of conditions, including the size and distance of the light source. For this reason, cast shadows are generally not the best indicators of form, but they can be very useful in giving clues to an object's surroundings. For example, one clue they provide is how far from another object, or background, the object casting the shadow is located. Look at Figure 7.7 and you can quite obviously tell which sphere is closer to the wall and even which sphere is larger.

FIGURE 7.7   Both size and position in space can be determined by an object's cast shadow.

Cast shadows can also give you important clues about where an object is in the environment and in relationship to the viewer. In Figure 7.8, the shadow cast by the object gives you valuable information as to where the object is in relation to the viewer, even when the object casting the shadow is out of view.

FIGURE 7.8   An example of the ability of a shadow to reveal important information about the object casting the shadow, even though the object is out of the field of view. You can easily surmise several things about the object, including both its position and intent.

A second use of value is the expressive. Is your work predominantly light or dark? A dark image would be appropriate if you wanted to create moody effects such as danger or sadness. On the other hand, a light image would be more appropriate for images with the opposite types of feelings. Figure 7.9 shows an example of both a predominantly light and a predominantly dark image.

FIGURE 7.9   Images that are predominantly light or dark.

A third use of value is decorative. Using values decoratively eliminates the need for a light source in a conventional sense. This approach works best with nonrepresentational or decorative art types, as shown in Figure 7.10.

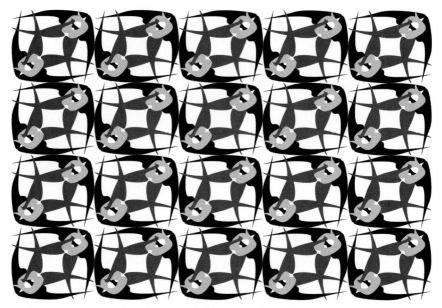

FIGURE 7.10   A pattern that shows the decorative use of value.

HOW TO USE VALUE EFFECTIVELY IN YOUR ART

So, what can you do to use value to your best advantage to create easily understandable and visually dynamic art? This section suggests several ideas.

Advancing and receding. First and foremost, light values generally appear to advance, and dark values appear to recede, as shown in Figure 7.11.

Locating the center of interest. Your center of interest will always be in the light or the lightest part of a dark piece, as shown in Figure 7.12.

Massing your values. Try to form an interlocking and underlying value pattern in your work to give it a sense of solidity and structure, as shown in Figure 7.13. Notice how the left side of the image looks disjointed because of the randomly placed elements. Then notice how the right half has some solidity because the elements begin to interlock and form value patterns.

FIGURE 7.11   This image shows how values can be used to change an object's visual location within an image.

FIGURE 7.12   Keeping the lightest values and greatest contrasts in the center of interest.

FIGURE 7.13   Massing value as opposed to random placement.

Expressing a mood. Have your work predominantly light or dark, depending on the mood and feeling you are trying to express. Avoid as much as possible too even a balance between the lights and darks. Figure 7.14 shows an image that is too equally balanced in value to be visually exciting.

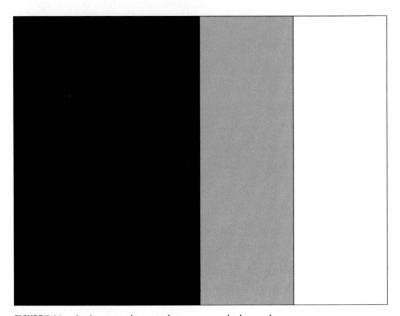

FIGURE 7.14   An image whose values are too balanced.

Getting the balance right. Too much balance generally leads to visually boring work. If you are having problems deciding how much dark and light value to have in your work, consider this generality. Have 60 percent of your work fall within the mid-range values, have 25 percent be either light or dark, and have the remaining 15 percent be the opposite, as shown in Figure 7.15.

FIGURE 7.15   A formula for balancing the proportions of value in an image.

Having a full range of value within your image. If your piece is predominantly light, make sure that there is still an area where you have some very darks. A wide range of value will help add the drama and contrast that is so needed in visually stimulating art.

There are situations where limiting the range of value would be appropriate. High key images would have most, if not all, of their values fall in a lighter range and would not have many, if any, darks. An example of a high key image might be a strongly lit landscape. Often, portrait images are also high key where the only darks are the eyes. Low key images are the opposite, where most the values are limited to darker values. Night scenes would generally be considered low key images. Both high and low key images usually have a limited contrast range.

Using contrasts. As value contrasts increase, color contrasts decrease.

Using intense colors. The most intense colors will usually be on the terminating edge between the light and dark, as shown in Figure 7.16. Here is a blue sphere being lit by a bright light. Notice that the parts of the sphere in the direct light are washed out to white, and the parts of the sphere in the shadow are black. The only area where you see the true and bright color of the sphere is on the edge between the light and dark.

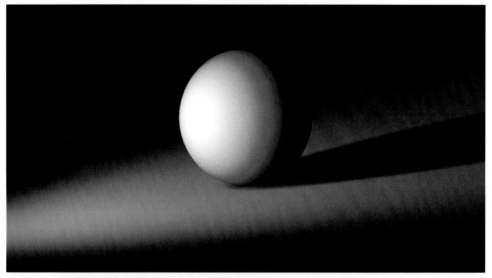

FIGURE 7.16   A blue sphere lit by a bright light showing the color on the terminating edge between the light and shadow.

Using gradation of light. As an object moves from near a light source to farther away, the light on that object will become gradually and slightly less intense, as shown in Figure 7.17.

Drawing attention to the focal point. Use your greatest value changes possible at your most important center of interest. Then gradually decrease those value changes as you move away from that focal point.

Using crisp changes. Keep your crispest changes between values at your centers of interest.

Transitioning. Keep your transitions between colors of the same value soft unless you want a cutout look. In animations, the movement will do this visually.

Using shadows. Warm lights need cool shadows; cool lights need warm shadows. Make sure that your shadows are consistent with the object they are associated with. For example, a light object will have a lighter shadow than a dark object's shadow.

FIGURE 7.17   An example of a light shining on a wall. Where the light is closest to the wall, the light is most intense when compared with the light on portions of the wall that are more distant from the light.

Using reflected lights. Do not let reflected lights punch visual holes into your shadows. Unless you are striving for some special effect, the reflected lights should disappear when you squint at your art.

Using counterchange. Make sure that the "light" areas in your shadows are darker than the "dark" areas in your lights. A mid-value in a light area will look dark and vice versa, as shown in Figure 7.18. This is the principle of counterchange. Counterchange is a function of simultaneous contrast. Basically, counterchange is the impression that a mid-value seen simultaneously against both a light and dark ground will appear light where it is against the dark and dark where it is against the light.

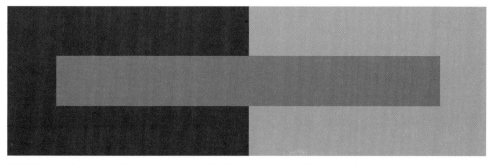

FIGURE 7.18   Identical values may look dark in lighter areas or light in dark areas.

RULES FOR USING VALUE IN YOUR IMAGES

If you remember the following "rules" and apply them to your images, your work will show immediate improvement:

- Value is about relationships.
- Form is described by value.

- Nothing is more important than value in picture making.
- There are two value areas in pictures: things that face the light source (lights) and things that face away from the light source (darks).
- Mid-values are a convenient way of tying together our lights and darks and will help us create pictures that are closer to the way we see. Imagine that your mid-values are everything that is not very light or very dark. When designing your picture, try to do the basic value plan using just three values. A general guide to follow when laying out your value pattern is this: 60 percent of your values should be in the mid-value range, 25 percent should be either light or dark, and the remaining 15 percent should be the opposite. The more complicated an image is, the simpler the overall value structure should be.
- Local value is the inherent lightness or darkness of an object.
- Atmospheric value is the idea that objects of similar local value will have different atmospheric values as they recede in the picture.
- Side light value is when an object's local value will change either lighter or darker when lit from an angle.
- Simultaneous contrast causes an object's local value to appear to move toward the opposite extremes when viewed adjacent to surrounding values.
- A light image is called high key, and a dark image is called low key.
- Artists tend to paint things too dark. It is easier to make the value darker than lighter. If you are not sure if the value is dark or mid-value, make it mid-value. If you are not sure what the difference between a light value and mid-value is, make it a light one.
- Work in simple values. Limit yourself to three values when you are planning out your compositions. This will help you arrange and organize your image without being caught up in unimportant detail.
- Stick to your original value plan. There is no limit to the amount of detail that you can have within a form if the form is the correct value locked into place within the composition.
- Detail is always subordinate to the overall value pattern of the composition. Detail is only incidental and descriptive.
- Keep your highest contrast between values at your center of interest.
- Value passages are important ways of unifying your pictures.
- Interlock your lights or darks.
- Use chiaroscuro to simplify your light and dark patterns. Chiaroscuro is defined as the technique of using light and shade in pictorial representation or the arrangement of light and dark elements in a pictorial work of art.
- Values on objects will gradually darken and have less contrast as they get farther away from the light source.
- Values that are in your light areas should never be as dark as the lightest areas of your darks, and vice versa.

- As value contrasts increase, color decreases. The brightest colors in your pictures may be found in the mid-values.
- The brightest colors in an object will be found in the transition edges between the lights and darks.

CONCLUSION

There is nothing more important in making art visually understandable than value. This chapter has touched briefly on ways that you can make value work for you to make your images visually stunning and understandable. In the next chapter, we will be discussing what is probably the second most important principle in creating art: color.

8

COLOR AND ITS USE IN PICTURE MAKING

S econd only to value is the importance of color. Color, above and beyond all other artistic principles, is the most seductive and most expressive. We all react immediately to color. It is what we use to fire emotions in our art. Color is probably the most studied and hardest to master of all the elements of art.

This chapter quickly covers some general color concepts that you have probably heard before. This review is important because many of us could be better with our use of color. Though this chapter is not about doing exercises, you can duplicate all of these examples using virtually any piece of 2D software.

THE FOUR PRIMARY CHARACTERISTICS OF COLOR

Color has four easily seen, understood, and measured characteristics. It is absolutely critical that all visual artists understand these characteristics.

Hue

Hue is fairly straightforward. Hue is the base color; it is red, blue, or any other color that you can name. In light, a color can have only one hue. A light's color corresponds directly with the hue wavelength in the spectrum, as shown in Figure 8.1.

FIGURE 8.1   The colors of the spectrum are represented by individual hues.

The only way to change a color's hue is to mix it with another color. Mixing colors results in a completely new hue with an entirely different wavelength. Working on a computer screen is exactly the opposite of working in paint. In light, your primary colors are red, blue, and green, with your secondary colors being yellow, magenta, and cyan. Light color is an additive process where the addition of all colors will result in white light. Paint colors, on the other hand, are a subtractive process where the addition of color darkens and lessens the effect of light. Theoretically, the addition of all paint colors will result in black. Paint primaries are red, yellow, and blue, with the secondary colors being orange, green, and violet.

Value

The value of a color is either how light or dark a color is. A color's value can be a tricky thing to understand. Some color value is easy to understand. When a blue's value is raised, and the color gets lighter, we still recognize the resulting color as blue. Red, on the other hand, is different. When we lighten the value of red, we get an entirely different color that we know as pink. The change of a color's value is shown in Figure 8.2.

FIGURE 8.2   A color's value is represented by how dark or light that color appears.

Chroma

For some, the concept of chroma seems to be very hard to grasp. Chroma is simply the intensity of the hue, as shown in Figure 8.3. As a color approaches a neutral gray, it is decreasing in chroma.

FIGURE 8.3   Chroma is represented by how gray a color looks.

Temperature

Color temperature (shown in Figure 8.4) is the most difficult of these four concepts to understand because it can be so relative. Usually, we think that the warm colors are yellow, orange, and red and the cool colors are green, blue, and violet. The reality is that depending on the surroundings, any color can be either warm or cool.

FIGURE 8.4   Temperature is represented by how warm or cool a color appears.

SECONDARY COLOR CHARACTERISTICS

While the secondary characteristics of color are a little harder to define, they are no less important to artists as they strive for good art.

Color Quality

Color quality is the effect of two or more colors reflected from a visually monochromatic surface. Color quality brings color to life and gives it a richness and sensuality. Take the blue squares in Figure 8.5 and compare them. The square with the subtle patterning appears much more visually exciting than the plain blue square.

FIGURE 8.5   Two squares of color with the same value; however, one is boring and flat, whereas the other shows good color quality.

Color Distance

Visually, colors appear to either come forward or recede in the picture plane. This appearance is called color distance. Warm colors appear to come forward, while cool colors tend to recede. Cool colors will recede even more if their edges are soft, as shown in Figure 8.6.

FIGURE 8.6   An illustration of color distance.

Color Weight

Color has a visual weight. Generally, the darker the color, the heavier it appears; and vice versa, the lighter the color, the lighter in weight it appears to be. A color's weight has two uses: to preserve balance and to express a visual mood. A dark color expresses strength and solidity, while a light color expresses delicacy and lightness, as shown in Figure 8.7.

FIGURE 8.7   Color weight.

HOW COLOR ACTS AND REACTS

This section briefly discusses how color interacts with other colors. If you know what to expect when painting, you will be able to make color work for you; you won't have to rely on happy accidents and unhappy disasters. All color is affected by surrounding color. The influence of surrounding colors brings up an interesting facet of color interaction: simultaneous contrast.

Simultaneous Contrast

The basic theory of simultaneous contrast is that differing colors placed next to each other will enhance their differences. If you have an orange square and place it next to a red field of color, it will look more yellow. The reverse is also true: that same orange on a field of yellow will look redder, as shown in Figure 8.8.

FIGURE 8.8   Simultaneous contrast between equally intense colors.

Another example of simultaneous contrast is a color surrounded by a field of gray. If the color is green, the gray will look redder; if the color is red, that same gray will look greener, as shown in Figure 8.9.

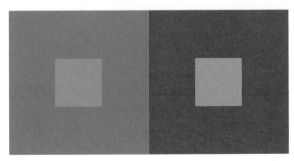

FIGURE 8.9   Simultaneous contrast between intense color and gray.

Color Contrast

Color contrast is simultaneous contrast in action. Often when you are painting, the color you are using will start to do some unusual things. This is generally because of color contrast. This is especially noticeable if you are painting within a gradient, as shown in Figure 8.10. The middle rectangle is one color, but because of the gradient that it is painted into, its visual look changes dramatically.

FIGURE 8.10   The figure represents what could happen if you are not careful choosing your colors. The middle rectangle is one color, but because of the colors that it is painted in to, its visual look changes dramatically.

USING COLORS EFFECTIVELY

Enough color theory. Here are some ideas to help you use colors more effectively when creating art:

- **Do not use your colors at full strength all over your art.** Reserve your colors of strongest intensity for your centers of interest. Color used all over at full strength will either bore or confuse your audience.
- **Decide who the audience for the picture is and choose the colors accordingly.** Be aware of gender, age, and education-level preferences.
- **Different color schemes call for different handling.** If you use a color scheme that is predominantly one color, or a family of colors, make sure that you also use a complementary color somewhere in your composition. (Near the center of interest is good.)
- **If you have large fields of one flat color, break it up using "noise."** Large expanses of flat colors are visually boring.
- **Establish your color scheme quickly and stick to it.** An established color scheme will help you keep from nitpicking individual elements and fracturing the color harmony.
- **Make sure that the colors look bright.** To make a color look brighter, place its complement next to it.
- **Use a color's tendency to advance or retreat to your benefit.** Warm color advances; cool color recedes.

Avoid colors that are hard to read. Pure blue should be avoided for text, thin lines, and small shapes. Also avoid adjacent colors that differ only in the amount of blue. Avoid red and green at the edge of large images.

A color's four main characteristics are subject to change. Colors change in appearance as the ambient light level changes.

When you are changing from one color to another, it is difficult to focus on edges created by color changes alone.

Conclusion

Never forget that, first and foremost, artists are doing something visual. People must be able to see what you are doing and then be able to grasp what you are saying. That is why it is so important to understand the basic principles of visual art, with value and color being the most critical. In the next chapter, we will be discussing an artistic principle that is linked closely with both value and color: lighting.

USING LIGHTING ARRANGEMENTS TO LIGHT A CHARACTER EFFECTIVELY

You may be wondering why a book primarily concerned with 2D painting has a chapter with examples of 3D lighting. The reason is quite simple: it is very easy to use 3D examples to describe lighting arrangements and how they work, and then explain how to apply that knowledge to 2D images. If you understand lighting, your painted and sketched images will have more strength and believability.

Some excellent and detailed books on lighting are available online or in bookstores. This chapter is not meant to supplant such valuable resources or be an all-inclusive and in-depth discussion on how to light characters or show specific positions for placing lights in 3D space. It is only a simplified overview of different lighting arrangements that are effective and have been used by traditional photographers and artists throughout the ages.

This chapter does not assume that you know a thing about 3D programs, nor is knowledge of 3D applications necessary to understand the lighting principles presented.

All of us know the importance of lighting in our images. Many times, though, artists will not give lighting much thought. Confusing and/or boring lighting schemes are usually the result.

You must remember that the casual viewer may not be the most visually astute viewer, and confusing lighting will be just as bad as boring lighting when you are trying to make your point. Good, careful lighting will help you flesh out your ideas and make them understandable. Most often, you will be using lighting as the main tool to create mood and feeling.

Look through this chapter for inspiration when you are struggling with how to light your subject or how to portray a specific mood. Look at the different lighting arrangements that are presented, and you will surely find something to help you preserve and enhance the mood you are attempting to evoke when painting your character.

A basic blueprint for each lighting arrangement is given so that when you are lighting models in either 3D or real life, you will have a starting reference point to work with. Specific heights and distances from the model are not given because each individual situation requires individual attention.

Using Lighting to Create Striking Art

The most important thing when you are using lighting to create something striking—and not boring or lackluster—is to be sure of what you are trying to create. You should consider all of the following questions when planning the lighting of your character:

> **What mood do you want to create?** Do you want to create a peaceful, ominous, theatrical, or outer space effect? The mood you want will to a large degree determine where you place your lights.
>
> **Do you want your lighting to be harsh or soft?** A rainy day would not lend itself to any harsh direct light.

What colors should your lights be? Do you want your scene to be predominantly hot or cold, or light or dark? Obviously, a dark blue light will make a darker scene. Remember that a colored light will affect all colors in a scene.

The Main Types of Lighting

The lighting arrangements presented in the next few sections will give you ideas about lighting a scene effectively. These arrangements could be used either in 3D applications or when you're shooting reference material from living models.

Main or Key Light

Traditionally, the most desirable light for painting or drawing has been high, north light. This light is a cool, soft light that defines form well. In our computer world, this is also good place to start. Position your light source on a 45-degree angle from your line of sight to your target. Where you position this light source in the vertical plane should be determined by the mood that you want. It should be higher for a more natural look, and lower for a more theatrical look. This light should be the brightest. Figures 9.1 and 9.2 show two kinds of key lights.

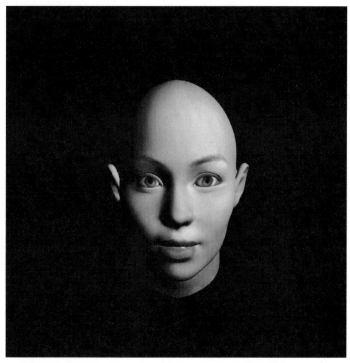

FIGURE 9.1   The key light is positioned high relative to the head.

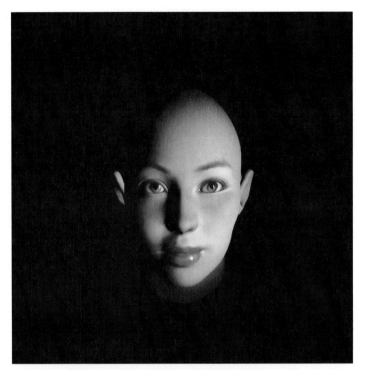

FIGURE 9.2   The key light is positioned at head level.

Secondary or Fill Light

Invariably, objects in the character's environment will reflect light into the shadows of the character. The atmosphere even does this to a certain degree. Possibly the only place where this would not happen is in deep space, where there is nothing to reflect the light back into the shadow. Yet, we have become so used to seeing this reflected light that it is represented even in space scenes. Reflected light, then, is why you will generally want a secondary light source. It's preferable to locate this light at the same vertical level or opposite angle level of the primary light, as shown in Figure 9.3.

Secondary light should be at a 50 percent or less intensity of the primary light source. It's a good idea to have your secondary light source be complementary to the primary light or neutral in color. Having a fill light that is too strong will, in most cases, begin to destroy the illusion of volume, killing form and punching visual holes into your object.

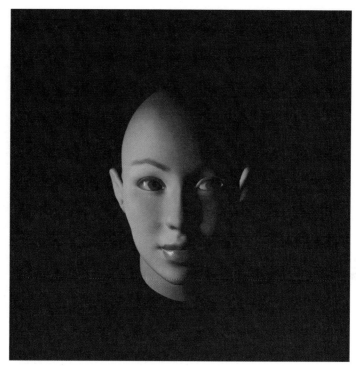

FIGURE 9.3   A secondary or fill light.

Rim Lights

If a light source is in your field of view, you will need a rim light on your object. Placing the light at 135 degrees from your line of sight is a good starting point. You do not see a lot of rim lighting in traditional painting, but it is used extensively in contemporary illustration. Rim lights lend a sparkle to an image while helping to define form, as shown in Figure 9.4.

Backlights

Backlights are used to separate your objects from your background. Backlights shine on the background object instead of your main object and should usually be just strong enough to separate your figure from the background. If your background light is too bright, it will tend to silhouette your figure and make it more 2D. Of course, this may be just what you want. Figure 9.5 shows a very typical backlighting situation.

FIGURE 9.4 A rim light.

FIGURE 9.5 A lighting setup using backlight.

Sunlight

Sunlight almost always has an equal in 3D programs. Remember that when you're trying to simulate direct sunlight in your scenes, the light needs to be kept very intense. In addition, it usually casts harsh, very high-contrast, shadows. Direct sunlight can vary from white to orange depending on the time of day you are trying to represent. Indirect sunlight, such as what you see on an overcast day, can have almost any color tinge and will generally cast very weak and soft shadows if any shadows are cast at all.

Ambient Light

Ambient light is usually not really a light source. Rather, it is usually the amount of light bouncing around an environment that illuminates an object. Clear, sunny days may not have as much ambient illumination as foggy days. The default ambient light settings of most programs tend to be too high. As a general rule, keep the ambient light settings of all the objects in your scene relatively close. If you find that the shadows in your art are just too dark and harsh, try increasing the ambient light settings.

Positioning Your Lights

This section contains some examples of lighting setups to give you starting places for your own explorations. These examples are directly applicable to drawing and painting.

Lighting at a 45-Degree Angle with One Light Source

Place your light at a 45-degree angle in relation to your line of sight. This lighting will produce high-contrast value patterns while doing a fairly good job of defining the target form. Almost unlimited lighting variations are available if you raise and lower the light source. Figures 9.6 and 9.7 show two examples of 45-degree lighting schemes.

Lighting at a 45-Degree Angle with Two Light Sources

The first light is the main light source, and the second is the fill light. This scenario is identical to the previous lighting arrangement except for the addition of the fill light. If you vary the brightness of the fill along with the vertical position of both lights, the variations and control possibilities are limitless. Figure 9.8 shows an example of a simple lighting scheme using two light sources.

FIGURE 9.6   An example of a very simple 45-degree lighting scheme.

FIGURE 9.7   Lighting at a 45-degree angle with one light source, but at a lower position.

Lighting at a 90-Degree Angle with One Light Source

The light is placed at a 90-degree angle from your line of sight. The light illuminates only half of your target, with the other half remaining in total darkness. This arrangement is not nearly as useful as when you use 45-degree lighting. With the 90-degree-angle scenario, form is harder to define, but you can get a nice ominous effect if that is what you are after. Again, vary the height of the light to get the feel you want. Figure 9.9 shows what happens when you are using one light source located at 90 degrees to the subject.

FIGURE 9.8   An example of lighting using two light sources.

FIGURE 9.9   Using a single light source located at 90 degrees to the subject.

In Figure 9.10, the side light is positioned at a relatively high angle to the model.

Lighting at a 90-Degree Angle with One 45-Degree-Angle Fill

The main reason for the use of the fill in this case is to lessen the abrupt transition from the darkness to the shadow. Figure 9.11 shows how a fill light will help bring out the details in the shadows.

FIGURE 9.10   Lighting at a 90-degree angle with one light source, but at a higher angle.

FIGURE 9.11   Adding one 45-degree-angle fill light to bring back detail in the shadows.

By placing the fill in the dark plane, as shown in Figure 9.12, you can add some detail back into your target. Vary the height to taste.

Lighting at a 135-Degree Angle

The light is placed almost behind your target. This kind of lighting is the almost ideal position for great rim lighting. Figure 9.13 shows the location of a light to produce rim lighting.

FIGURE 9.12   Lighting at a 90-degree angle with one 45-degree-angle fill in the dark side of the face.

FIGURE 9.13   Lighting at a 135-degree angle to produce rim light.

Lighting at Double 135 Degrees

Use this lighting if you want to produce silhouettes. Figure 9.14 shows an example of double rim lighting.

Front Lighting

Here, the light source is positioned very close to your line of sight. Front lighting will flatten whatever it is illuminating. Such lighting is not very useful when positioned at camera level. Figure 9.15 shows front lighting at the camera level.

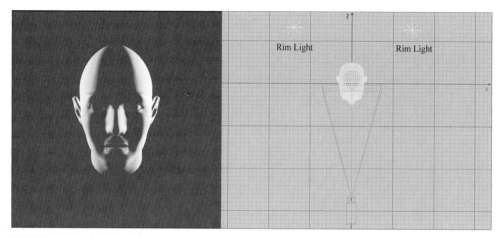

FIGURE 9.14   Double rim lighting.

FIGURE 9.15   Front lighting at the camera level.

If you raise and lower the front light, good things can happen. Get the light high enough and you will get a good approximation of Rembrandt-style lighting, as shown in Figure 9.16.

If you lower the light, you will get a theatrical look that can be quite ominous if you want it to be, as shown in Figure 9.17.

FIGURE 9.16   Rembrandt-style lighting.

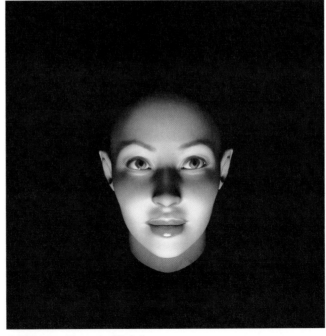

FIGURE 9.17   Theatrical lighting.

The Color of Your Lights

While it may seem obvious, you should nevertheless take great care when choosing the color of your lights. Color can enhance or destroy the effect that you are after. Figure 9.18 shows two rather unimpressive, checkered pill shapes lit by neutral white light.

FIGURE 9.18   A neutral white light.

Be aware of what similarly and complementary-colored lights will do to your objects. A red light will completely wash out and negate all the reds in your scene, making them appear as the whites. At the same time, a red light will make the green color appear as black, as shown in Figure 9.19.

Green lights will do exactly the opposite to your red colors, as shown in Figure 9.20.

Use colored lights where needed, especially for accent lights, but do not overuse them.

A Last Word About Shadows

One of the beauties of 3D programs is that you can determine which objects cast and receive cast shadows. If the cast shadows do not enhance the form of the objects

FIGURE 9.19   The effect of a red light.

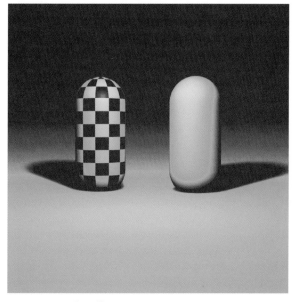

FIGURE 9.20   The effect of a green light.

they are falling on, as shown in Figure 9.21, it would probably be best to eliminate their use.

FIGURE 9.21   A cast shadow that destroys the form of the object that it is cast on.

The same reasoning holds true for 2D works. If a cast shadow does not enhance the form that it is falling on or if it is a distraction, it is usually best to eliminate it.

CONCLUSION

It is hoped that this chapter gave you some different lighting ideas to consider when you are painting your character. If you are lucky enough to use a 3D program when you are designing your character, you can experiment with these variations of lighting to get just the look you are after. If you are actually going to take pictures of a living model to use as the basis for your painting, these are good starting points. As a general rule, the simplest and most straightforward lighting schemes will convey your ideas the best. Too many lights will only be confusing. In the next chapter, we will be discussing one of the most misunderstood concepts in good picture making: handling edges and edge quality.

10

USING EDGES WHEN PAINTING A PICTURE

In Chapters 7 and 8, we discussed value and color as the two most important artistic principles when creating art and images. In Chapter 9, we discussed ways to use light effectively. This chapter deals with the main problem that artists have when using value and color. This problem is the edges, where differing values, colors, or both meet. You need to know how to depict the transition from one shape to the next within an image. The careful and intelligent placement of different shapes, and how you handle the edges, is at the core of successful picture making, whether decorative or representational. This chapter will discuss the different types of edges, their variations, their use, and common problems associated with edges when you are painting. While it is easy to describe the different types of edges found in art, there are no rules for their use. However, this chapter will offer some generalities that can help give you more confidence as you plan and execute your paintings so they will become better. This chapter shows how edges interact with each other in the painting process.

TYPES OF EDGES

You will find only five types of edges in most digital and traditional art. Not all of the different edges will always be found in each painting, but obviously there will always be at least one kind of edge present in every work of art. The five types are as follows:

Rough/ragged edges. Rough edges are quite possibly the most noticeable of all the edge types and will be hard to miss when in an image. An example is shown in Figure 10.1. Depending on the technique, rough edges may be the most common type of edge within a painting. Traditionally, they are usually created using a dry-brush technique. They are much easier to create in the digital world and in just about every raster application.

FIGURE 10.1 An example of a rough and/or ragged edge.

Razor-sharp edges. Razor-sharp edges are visually the harshest edge. An example is shown in Figure 10.2. They have a very distinct cutout appearance, as if you cut out a shape and simply laid it down on the picture plane. Traditionally, this type of edge is relatively difficult to create unless you are using some sort of masking technique. These edges are easy to create digitally and can be created by both raster and vector applications. Their use is mainly in decorative art and, in a limited way, within representational painting.

FIGURE 10.2   An example of a razor-sharp edge.

Hard edges. Hard edges are just as the name suggests. An example is shown in Figure 10.3. They have a hard appearance, though not necessarily a cutout appearance. These edges will not be the most common edge found in most paintings, but they usually will be present. They are useful in attracting attention to your center of interest.

Soft edges. Soft edges are the most common type of edge found in paintings. An example is shown in Figure 10.4. They are the most common edge because there is so much variation in their size and how they are painted. They vary in width from being almost hard to being non-edges. As with all edges, you need to know how to use them to be successful at digital painting. These edges have numerous looks. You can create them within different raster applications, but you can only imitate them in vector programs.

Non-edges or lost edges. The last type of edge is not really an edge at all; rather, it is more like the lack of an edge. An example is shown in Figure 10.5. As we look at the world around us, we see many instances where there are no definable edges between separate objects. This may be a function of

FIGURE 10.3 An example of a hard edge.

FIGURE 10.4 An example of a soft edge.

the lighting, the amount of time that we have to look at an object, the object's distance, or any number of other reasons. If you do not see an edge, why paint an edge? This seems to be one of the hardest concepts for artists to grasp. For some reason, people seem to want to compartmentalize the world around them, and this means that individual objects have a contour. While intellectually we all know that this is true, this is not always the case visually. The lack of an edge can best be represented by an even gradation. These non-edges are some of the easiest effects to create in digital painting programs, yet their use is avoided.

FIGURE 10.5   An example of a non-edge.

HOW EDGES INTERACT

When you're working with edges, you need to consider the following:

- What happens when there are numerous edges and transitions of either value or color within your painting?
- Which edges and transitions will be noticed first?
- How do you visually control which edges are noticed and which are not?

Edges and Value

Value will most often determine which edge is visually dominant in a composition. Edges with the greatest value differences have the most visual impact, as shown in Figure 10.6. This holds true in almost all cases. A soft edge between widely different values will have more impact than a ragged edge between closer values.

FIGURE 10.6   Edges of greater value difference are visually more dramatic and eye catching than edges with less contrast.

Similarly painted edges will not always have the same visual impact, as you can see in Figure 10.7, where identical edges are changed only in the value contrasts between them. Those of greater contrast are visually more exciting than those of lesser contrast.

FIGURE 10.7   Differing visual impact between identically blended edges.

Although the edges in the example are of an identical roughness, the value between the adjacent edges is critical. Quite obviously, the more contrast there is in an edge (no matter what type of edge), the more noticeable that edge will be. While the comparison in this example is extreme, the principle nevertheless holds true.

Edges and Color

Color hue differences will control how much visual impact there is in an edge. Intense complementary colors will give the most visually dominant edges, as shown in Figure 10.8.

FIGURE 10.8   Two intense complementary hues will give dramatic edges.

Unfortunately, intense complementary hued edges are dramatic as well as tiring to the eye. Hence, you should use them with great care and in small areas. Edges where one of the colors is less intense yet still complementary will still give dramatic edges but with less visual fatigue, as shown in Figure 10.9.

FIGURE 10.9   An edge formed by intense and muted complementary hues.

The edge formed between two neutralized hues will be the least dramatic of the complementary combinations, as shown in Figure 10.10.

FIGURE 10.10   Two subdued complementary hues that form an edge are not as dramatic as more intense combinations.

Analogous colored edges will be less noticeable than edges created with complementary colors, as shown in Figure 10.11. This holds true even when both edges are created with intense hues.

FIGURE 10.11   An edge formed by analogous colors compared to an edge formed by complementary colors.

Analogous colors that have different color temperatures will have more noticeable edges than analogous colors with similar color temperatures, as shown in Figure 10.12.

FIGURE 10.12   Edge differences between analogous colors of different temperatures.

Color intensity will also affect how we see edges. The edge between two equally intense colors will be very dramatic and visually intense, as shown in Figure 10.13. Such an edge will be visually tiring unless used only in small areas.

FIGURE 10.13   An edge between two equally intense and bright colors.

The edge between an intense color and a neutral color will not be as dramatic, as shown in Figure 10.14.

FIGURE 10.14   An edge between an intense and bright color and a more neutral color.

The least dramatic edge is that based on color intensities between neutral and subdued hues, as shown in Figure 10.15.

FIGURE 10.15   An edge between two very neutral colors.

WHERE YOU WILL FIND THE DIFFERENT TYPES OF EDGES

The following suggestions are intended to help you decide where you want to place different edges, where to look for edges, and how to use the different edge qualities to advantage in your work. You will use edges to lead viewers through your picture and to get them to look at the areas you want as well as in the order that you want them to be looked at. Here are some things to keep in mind:

Place your most interesting and visually dominant edges at the center of interest. The most intense and dominant edges are generally the ragged, razor sharp, and sharp ones. Place these in the following areas:
- The center of interest
- Areas that are in direct light
- The cast shadow of an object closest to the object itself
- The edges of angular objects in your picture
- An area where the local hue changes but the values remain the same, and vice versa
- Thin objects
- Wherever you want a very flat, 2D effect, or a decorative effect

You will see some edges before others. Use this to your advantage when planning your painting. You will see a light edge against the dark before you will see an edge made of mid-values. You will see a hard edge before you will see a soft edge. You will see non-edges last, if at all.

Soft edges are not noticed nearly as much as the harsher ones. Use this type of edge in the following places:
- Areas of your image that are not in the center of interest
- Background areas

- The shadow areas of your painting
- Areas that are lit by diffuse, soft, and indirect lights
- Cast shadows as they move away from the object that is casting the shadow
- The edges of objects that are receding in the picture plane
- Turning edges of organic forms
- Where local values change and/or local colors change
- Where you need help uniting the figure and background

Non-edges are hardly noticeable, if perceived at all. Keep the following in mind:

- Non-edges are found generally in the shadow areas and areas of least interest.
- Non-edges will help keep the shadows from becoming too noticeable.
- Non-edges will provide smooth transitions for both color and value in the shadow areas.
- Non-edges can be used to provide an area of mystery.
- Most important, non-edges can help hide your mistakes.

CONCLUSION

This is an important chapter. Edges and how you handle them in your character design will be one thing that separates your work from the ordinary. Now, we hope, you know the types of edges, where they are found, and how to use them. In Chapter 11, we will start to transition away from theory into some of the more practical aspects of painting; we will discuss blending the edges in your digital painting.

11

BLENDING EDGES IN YOUR DIGITAL PAINTINGS

B lending your edges and colors in digital painting programs is not hard. Maybe it is actually too simple. In most programs, the default Airbrush tool makes it very, very easy to make gradated transitions between colors. It also makes it extremely easy to get soft edges. Some painting programs, Photoshop included, also offer a smudge or smear tool. Some talented artists use only these tools and get marvelous results. However, for the majority of digital artists, these tools leave a sterile and soulless handling of blended color and edges.

This chapter will show you two distinct things: a new method of blending color and edges using Photoshop and a method that does not really blend but gives the impression of blending.

One of the beautiful things about traditional painting is that for the most part the strokes that blend the different colors together are visible. Although this chapter is not about trying to duplicate the traditional blending of strokes, for the most part, the image you are painting will be much more interesting if you can see some color variations in your blended areas.

A New Method for Blending the Edge Where Your Colors and Shapes Meet

This method of blending color and edges together is so simple that it really does not merit a chapter to itself, yet the technique you are going to learn is new to most digital artists. It is the method that I use for almost all blending tasks when painting in Photoshop.

The success of this method is achieved not by using any of the default Photoshop brushes or even via a combination of any of the regular tools that are used to blend. This method is based on using Photoshop's tools in new and innovative ways. It is hoped that by seeing how some common tools are used in new ways, your imagination and desire to experiment will be sparked.

Now on to blending color in Photoshop in a new and unique way. Figure 11.1 shows the image we will use as the basis for the exercise.

We intentionally chose colors from all over the color wheel because such complementary colors are inherently more difficult to blend well. As you try this technique, create an image similar to this one or use the image provided on the CD-ROM.

ON THE CD

To use this method to blend colors in Photoshop, you need to do some preliminary work. The nice thing is that after you have done these few steps the first time, you will not have to repeat them the next time you use this technique.

First, create a new image of any small size. Typically, anything from 32 × 32 pixels square to 128 × 128 pixels is fine. There is no reason for it to be larger. Fill the image with any color you want, or just leave the default background color (white).

In the Edit menu, scroll down and click the Define Pattern menu item, as shown in Figure 11.2.

FIGURE 11.1   The image that will be used to blend color.

FIGURE 11.2   The Define Pattern menu item.

This brings up a dialog box asking you to name your new pattern, along with a preview image of your pattern. Your preview image should look either completely white or consist of the solid color you used to fill your original image.

Go ahead and close the image you used to create your pattern. There is no need to save that image.

Now the magic begins. Pick the Healing Brush tool from the toolbar. It is the one that looks like a small adhesive bandage. Figure 11.3 shows the Healing Brush.

FIGURE 11.3   The Healing Brush tool.

When the Healing Brush is selected, the options for the tool appear in the Tool Options bar at the top of the page. The size of the Healing Brush should be adjusted to suit the size of the area that you are going to blend. The larger the area, the larger the tool setting. If the brush size is particularly small, say smaller than 10, you may want to increase the size no matter how small the area you will blend. Leave the Mode setting at its default. The Source setting will default to Sampled; change this to

Pattern by clicking in the small circle to the right of the word Pattern. You will now see a thumbnail appear of the currently active pattern. Click on the small down arrow next to the thumbnail and select the blank or colored pattern you created. The Healing Brush is now set to be a blending tool.

In the open image, zigzag a stroke across the borders of the colors. Do not pay any attention to the color of the stroke. In Figure 11.4 you will notice that the stroke appears white.

FIGURE 11.4   The Healing Brush stroke appears to be white.

This is because the pattern that is being used is white. If the pattern were black or some other color, the stroke would appear either as black or as a color.

As soon as you lift the brush, the color will disappear, and you will see a nicely blended stroke, as shown in Figure 11.5.

Quite obviously, one stroke is not going to be enough to get a good blend, so go over the area again until you get just the amount of blending that you want. Notice how much softer and controlled the blend is when multiple strokes have been used, as shown in Figure 11.6.

Experiment with different widths of strokes and brush sizes. The narrower you stroke, the smaller the blend, and, conversely, the larger you stroke, the larger and smoother the blend between the two colors will be. You can see the results of both small blending strokes in Figure 11.7.

FIGURE 11.5 A nicely blended stroke.

FIGURE 11.6 Softer strokes result when you use multiple blends.

FIGURE 11.7   Large and small blending strokes.

There you have it: the best blending tool in Photoshop made from a tool that was not meant to be a blender.

Let's play with the shape of the brush a bit and see what happens to the blend. Figure 11.8 shows the options for the Healing Brush at the default settings.

FIGURE 11.8   The default Healing Brush.

One of the first things you can change is the Hardness setting. A lower setting will give your stroke a more feathered edge. The other settings will have a more distinctive effect on the way the brush behaves. Let's change the settings to look like Figure 11.9.

FIGURE 11.9   The modified Healing Brush.

Zigzag on the border between the two colors. Your stroke will look something like the one shown in Figure 11.10.

When you lift your stroke, you will notice that the color is still blending but not quite as smoothly. The amount of blend will once again depend on how many strokes you overlap on each other. Figure 11.11 shows the result of the stroke using the new brush settings for the Healing Brush tool.

Another way to vary the way the colors are blended using the Healing Brush other than changing the brush settings is to change and adjust the pattern you are using. Here, subtlety is a blessing. If you have a pattern that is too distinctive, you will get something that looks like Figure 11.12. The colors are not blending, and the pattern takes over the stroke.

Let's create a pattern that will help enhance the blending of colors but not become overpowering. Create a new image as you did earlier in the chapter. In this case, a little larger image is easier to work with than a smaller one, so make your image somewhere between 128 × 128 pixels and 256 × 256 pixels.

FIGURE 11.10   The stroke using the adjusted brush.

FIGURE 11.11   Result of the stroke using the new brush.

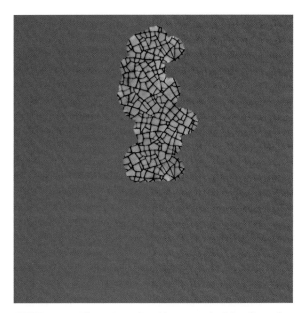

FIGURE 11.12   The pattern is taking over the blending of the colors.

In the Filter menu, apply the filter Render Clouds. Figure 11.13 shows the result.

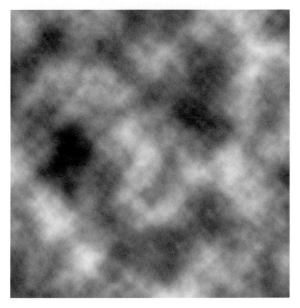

FIGURE 11.13   The Render Clouds filter applied to the image.

In the Image menu, select Adjustments > Brightness and Contrast, and check the Use Legacy box as shown in Figure 11.14.

FIGURE 11.14   Choosing Brightness and Contrast from the menu.

You want to end up with an image that is so subtle in its contrast range that it is a little hard to see the differences. Save the pattern as you did earlier in the chapter. Using the Healing Brush and your new pattern, blend the colors in your image. If you have created a pattern that is subtle enough, you will have a very nice blend with a slight unevenness. Figure 11.15 shows the blended image with some unevenness in the result.

FIGURE 11.15   The blended image created using a pattern with some noise in it.

Often this type of unevenness is preferable to a smoother blend in art. Areas that are too smooth appear boring to the eye, whereas areas with some texture will hold visual interest longer. After all, isn't holding the viewers' attention what all artists want?

You should also notice that the Healing Brush is in a menu that has more than one tool associated with the icon. Click the Bandage icon and hold down your mouse button. You will notice that two other tools are available. One of them, the Color Replacement tool, is really of no use when blending with this technique, but the other one has some magic in it. The Patch tool can also be used to blend color, though in a less "painterly" way than with the Healing Brush. Choose the Patch tool and notice that Photoshop updates the toolbar with a new icon that loosely resembles a patch, as shown in Figure 11.16.

FIGURE 11.16   The Patch tool icon.

Make sure that the pattern you created is again the active pattern. Draw with the Patch tool and notice that it acts like the Lasso tool in that it creates a selection. In fact, you can hold down the Shift key to add more to the selection and the Alt key to take away from the selection. Figure 11.17 shows a selection made using the Patch tool.

FIGURE 11.17   A selection made using the Patch tool.

When you have finished making your selection, click the Use Pattern button and see what happens. As you can see, your colors are evenly blended. In fact, they are much more evenly blended than can be done by hand. The larger the selection, the larger the blend will be. Figure 11.18 shows colors blended using the Patch tool.

Another way to enhance interest when blending colors is to add a small band of color between adjacent colors, as shown in Figure 11.19.

When you blend these colors, you will get an interesting and sometimes unpredictable result. There are two reasons for adding the band of color. One is to simply add some visual excitement to the image. The second is that sometimes when blending very complementary colors, this small band of color will make the transitions between the major colors visually smoother. Figure 11.20 shows the result of blending using a small middle band of color. Notice how the subtle greens add visual excitement to the image.

FIGURE 11.18 Colors blended using the Patch tool.

FIGURE 11.19 Adding a small band of color in between the two main colors.

FIGURE 11.20   Blending after adding a small band of color in between the two major colors.

OPTIONAL BLENDING METHOD

Many artists use another technique to give the impression of blending colors when painting in Photoshop. This method is fundamentally different than the previous method because instead of blending the color after you have painted, you paint to give the impression that you are blending the colors.

Much of the success of this technique depends on the brush that you pick to paint with. Though most brushes work, those with anti-aliased edges, or soft edges, will work the best. Also, brushes with the Other Dynamics box checked and an opacity jitter set to low will work very well. Figure 11.21 shows the Other Dynamics box checked and the opacity jitter set very low.

ON THE CD

The next series of figures demonstrate how this works and just how easy the technique is to use. Follow along to better understand. Begin by creating a new image or use the original image from this chapter provided on the CD-ROM.

Sample color from one side and paint into the other. Reselect color from the other side and paint back into the original side. Figure 11.22 shows colors from each side painted into the other color.

FIGURE 11.21   The Other Dynamics palette.

FIGURE 11.22   Colors sampled from each side of the image painted into the opposite side.

The important thing to notice is where the colors have painted over each other at less than 100% opacity. These areas are highlighted by the red arrows in the zoomed-in areas of Figure 11.23. These colors are important ones and are the ones you will sample with the eyedropper to continue painting. Figure 11.23 shows an extremely zoomed-in version of the previous painting showing the intermediate colors that you will now use to paint with.

FIGURE 11.23   The intermediate colors to paint with.

Sample some of the intermediate color and continue to paint on the edge. Notice that, as the strokes are built up, they become softer and softer. Continue to sample intermediate color and paint until you have nice smooth transitions between colors. Figure 11.24 shows the earlier image after additional painting on the edges using sampled intermediate colors.

FIGURE 11.24   Blending can be achieved using overlapping brush strokes.

This technique of painting using the intermediate colors created by individual brush strokes is the most widely used method of working in Photoshop. While this technique involves finding colors within the individual strokes and not blending existing pixels, it is an important method of painting with Photoshop. We included it in this chapter because the results are similar and are meant to emulate the blending of colors.

CONCLUSION

You can now see how easy it is to blend colors in Photoshop. Using these simple techniques will give your paintings a life that far exceeds the look that is possible using only the Airbrush or Smudge tools. In the next chapter, we will explore ways to use textures in your Photoshop paintings.

12

CREATING TEXTURES AND PATTERNS FOR USE IN DIGITAL PAINTING

When you're learning to paint on the computer, one of the most important skills you can master is being able to create and paint with texture. If you paint with texture, you can produce effects that would be tedious, if not impossible, to do with traditional methods. Not only are you able to create such effects, but you can do so quickly.

This chapter will show you how to go about creating custom textures from photographs by using Photoshop's Pattern Maker and by hand-drawing patterns. While these methods are demonstrated in Photoshop, most of the techniques shown are applicable to other painting applications.

Just so there is no confusion, within Photoshop, textures are called patterns. The terms are interchangeable for our purposes.

ON THE CD

In the Chapter 12 folder on the CD-ROM, you'll find a group of textures selected and created especially for this chapter.

CREATING TEXTURES

As when creating textures for 3D applications, you need to remember a few things when creating textures for use in 2D paint programs:

The size of the texture is important. 2D paint programs hold the texture in memory when you are using them to paint. Having somewhat smaller textures will increase the speed at which you can work. You can have and use large textures, and artists often do for specific projects. However, typically textures should be rather small, usually less than 512 × 512 pixels in dimension. More often than not, it's best to try to keep your textures 256 × 256 pixels in dimension.

Contrast is important. Most paint programs use the value information in an image to create the texture. Having images with narrow value ranges will not provide as effective textures as will images with a large range of values. The opposite can also be true. A strictly black and white image will often prove to be too "contrasty" and harsh.

Seamless is generally better. It's not very desirable to be in the middle of painting and suddenly have a line appear in your image where the texture ends. Try to always make the textures that you use seamless so that their edges will not become a distraction.

There are three main methods of creating textures in the digital world: taking and manipulating images from the real world; using computer applications, in this case Photoshop, that are capable of creating textures; and drawing your own by hand.

CREATING TEXTURES FROM PHOTOGRAPHIC REFERENCE MATERIALS

The main requirement for creating textures from photo reference is to be aware of your surroundings. If you cannot see the textural surfaces around you, you will not be able to use them. You might want to get in the habit of carrying a camera around with you. You never know when something will catch your eye and will be usable in an image you are contemplating.

You can use a digital camera to photograph the textures that you see around you. Film cameras as well as scanners are also useful. Whatever you use to get the image is really not important, as long as you get the image. An inexpensive digital camera will serve you just as well as an expensive one. Most of the inexpensive digital cameras now days have more than enough image resolution to be more than adequate for taking texture photographs. Digital is preferable because it is so easy to get the image into the computer. Figures 12.1 through 12.3 are digital pictures of some natural textures found in the canyon close to my home.

FIGURE 12.1   Texture number 1.

FIGURE 12.2   Texture number 2.

FIGURE 12.3 Texture number 3.

These images are good beginnings for drawing some great textures in your paintings, but they're not really usable in their current form. To get the images ready to be used as textures in Photoshop, follow these steps:

1. Pick any of the three images and resize it to approximately 400 × 300 pixels.
2. In the Filter menu, select Other and then Offset. In the resulting dialog box, offset the image 200 pixels in the horizontal direction and 150 pixels in the vertical direction. Make sure the circle next to Wrap Around is checked. Your image will now look like the one in Figure 12.4.

FIGURE 12.4 The texture with offset applied.

Now it is quite obvious where the seams of the image are located. With the sides of the image moved into the center, it is time to get rid of the seams and have a texture that can be tiled.

3. You can use several methods to get rid of these seams in Photoshop. Each has different strengths and weaknesses. You can use the Clone Stamp tool, the Healing Brush tool, and the feathered cut-and-paste technique. Usually a combination of all three will bring you the best results.

To use the cut-and-paste method, do the following. Using the rectangular selection tool, select a relatively thin selection of the image that is almost the whole vertical height of the image, as shown in Figure 12.5.

FIGURE 12.5   The tall, vertical selection.

Feather the selection about 5 pixels, and then copy and paste the selection. You can see the part that is copied and pasted in Figure 12.6.

Place this feathered selection over the middle seam of your image. Move it up or down to get a good random placement. Often you may need to paste several pieces to get good coverage of the vertical seam. When you have covered the vertical seam to your liking, merge down all the layers.

4. Now do the same thing in the horizontal direction. Make a long horizontal selection, feather the selection, copy it, and paste it back into the image. Figure 12.7 shows the horizontal selection that will be pasted back into the image.

FIGURE 12.6 The selection that is cut and pasted.

FIGURE 12.7 The feathered horizontal selection.

Once again, it might take more than one paste operation to cover the horizontal seam completely. Figure 12.8 shows the texture with all the seams now covered.

When the seams are covered to your satisfaction, go ahead and merge all the layers down.

FIGURE 12.8   The texture with both the horizontal and vertical seams covered.

5. Increase the contrast of the image, as shown in Figure 12.9. You can do this in Image > Adjustments > Brightness and Contrast or Image > Adjustments > Auto Contrast.

FIGURE 12.9   The texture with the contrast increased.

6. You will notice that there is still some unevenness in the image along the horizontal and vertical areas where the original seams were. This value difference needs to be minimized as much as possible or your image will appear distinctly repetitive when used as a pattern. A simple way to minimize these large value differences is by using the High Pass filter (from the Filter menu, choose Other and then choose High Pass). Figure 12.10 shows the High Pass filter slider with a radius setting of 20 pixels and the resulting change in the image.

Play with the slider until you remove as much of the value shift across the image as possible. The High Pass filter is extremely good at removing the low-frequency noise from images. You will notice that it also removes most of the color, but this is not really a concern when creating textures to paint with.

FIGURE 12.10   The texture with the High Pass dialog box displayed.

7. Run the Auto Levels adjustment to get a good range of values from dark to light. Figure 12.11 shows the texture after adjusting the levels.

8. Now let's save the newly created seamless texture as a pattern and have it available to use in your paintings. This is as simple as going to the Edit menu and selecting Define Pattern. Figure 12.12 shows the location of this command. Choosing it will bring up a dialog box asking what you want to call your new pattern. Call it whatever you like, but make it something you can remember. After defining your pattern, it is a good idea to go ahead and save the image you have been working with. You never know when you might need this image again.

FIGURE 12.11   The texture after running the Auto Levels command.

FIGURE 12.12   The Define Pattern
command found under the Edit menu.

Just as with brushes, when you have created a few of your own new and unique patterns, save them into your own pattern libraries.

PHOTOSHOP'S PATTERN MAKER

Photoshop 7, CS, CS2, and CS3 have a nifty little item nestled under the Filter menu called Pattern Maker. Pattern Maker has the potential of generating a virtually endless supply of seamless patterns. It uses information from either a selection within an image or the contents of the Clipboard. You can create multiple patterns from a single selection.

In this section, we will quickly go over creating various textures using Photoshop's Pattern Maker from a photographic reference.

ON THE CD

First, open any of the photographs of textures supplied on the CD-ROM. Select the Pattern Maker from the Filter menu, as shown in Figure 12.13.

FIGURE 12.13   The Pattern Maker.

You will notice that your cursor has turned into a crosshair. Use this to select a region with the image. You can move the selection around by clicking and holding within the selection.

After selecting the area you want to use to make the pattern, you need to tell Photoshop what size you want the seamless tile to be. These controls are found in the Tile Generation section of the Pattern Maker. You can have the tile be the whole image size, which will make the tiling image the same size as the original image. You can also enter numeric values in the width and height fields or drag the sliders that will pop up when you click on the small triangle to the right of the numbers.

If you want the tile to offset in either the vertical or horizontal direction, select Vertical or Horizontal in the Offset box. The default is No Offset. Below the Offset box is the amount of offset. This is a percentage of the pixel dimensions you specified.

Now, click the Generate button at the top of the Pattern Maker window. The preview area where the original texture or photo was displayed is now filled with the created pattern/texture, as shown in Figure 12.14.

FIGURE 12.14   The Pattern Maker window is filled with the generated pattern/texture.

The individual tile is displayed in the preview window in the Tile History section of the Pattern Maker. You can also preview the tile boundaries and how the individual tiles line up within the larger image by checking the Tile Boundaries box.

If you like the texture that is created, click on the small floppy icon right below the preview window. This will bring up the Pattern Name dialog box, shown in Figure 12.15.

FIGURE 12.15   The Pattern Name dialog box appears when you click on the small floppy logo below the preview window.

Name the pattern, and Photoshop will then save it into your current library. You can quickly generate an extremely large number of variations if you want by clicking the Generate Again button. As each pattern is generated, the preview will update. After a few (or many) patterns are generated, you can cycle through them using the arrows below the preview window. Save the ones you like and discard the ones you don't like by clicking on the small trash can icon. You can generate up to 20 tiles before the Pattern Maker begins to delete the oldest in the series.

Now you have seen two ways of creating seamless textures to use in your Photoshop painting projects. One more method worth mentioning is creating your textures by hand. While not the fastest method by any measure, it is the method where you have the most control over what you create. In the next section, you will see the general method used to create a texture by hand.

CREATING HAND-DRAWN TEXTURES FROM SCRATCH

This may become your favorite method for creating textures. The method is relatively straightforward and easy to master. The variety of textures possible is limited only by your imagination. Follow these steps to draw textures by hand using Photoshop:

1. Create a new image of any size up to about 600 × 600 pixels. Select any brush that you care to use and begin drawing and painting in the center of the image, as shown in Figure 12.16.

   In this particular case I am using the face7 brush. This brush can be found in the Brush library on the CD-ROM.

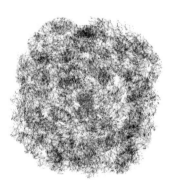

FIGURE 12.16   Begin painting in the texture, at first limiting your work to the center of the image.

2. In the Filter menu, select Other and then choose Offset. Make sure Wrap Around is selected and offset the image half its dimensions in both the vertical and horizontal directions. The image will have something of a cross shape in the middle, as shown in Figure 12.17.

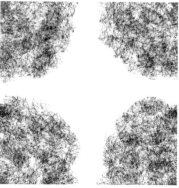

FIGURE 12.17   The texture offset in both the horizontal and vertical directions.

3. Continue to paint in the center of the image, working toward the edges but not touching them, as shown in Figure 12.18.

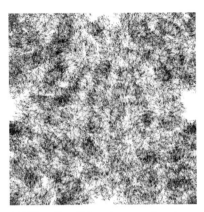

FIGURE 12.18   Using the same brushes and painting in the center of the image.

4. Once again, offset the image, but only one quarter of the dimensions this time. You now have only a couple of white areas located in opposite corners. Fill in these areas using your same brushes, as shown in Figure 12.19.

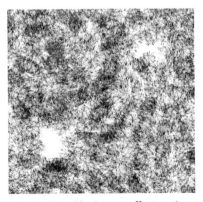

FIGURE 12.19   The image offset again, but only one quarter of the dimensions.

5. As Figure 12.20 shows, you now have a completely seamless texture that you can convert into a pattern and use in your painting.

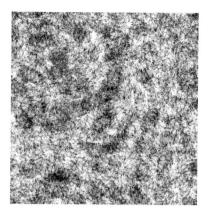

FIGURE 12.20   The completely hand-drawn custom texture.

CONCLUSION

This chapter has shown you three ways to create textures for use in digital paintings. There are, of course, as many ways of making textures as there are of creating digital art. The techniques shown here should be only a jumping off point for your own explorations. In the next chapter, we will go over Photoshop's powerful brushes. You will learn how to manipulate the default brushes to get them to behave as you would like, and you will learn how to create your own completely new, custom brushes.

PHOTOSHOP BRUSHES

SECTION 1: THE BASICS OF PHOTOSHOP BRUSHES

Many, many books have been published on how to use Photoshop. Because so many good materials are already available, we are not going to delve into all of the deep nooks and crannies of the program. This is a book on digital painting, and we will concentrate on what is most important to our task at hand: brushes and how to make them do what you want.

In this chapter, you will learn and/or refresh your memory on a number of different ways to access and use Photoshop's brushes. You will learn how to make a brush behave like you want. We will go over each of the palette and menu options that Photoshop gives you to control the look and feel of individual brushes. This will be a rather lengthy chapter, as we will look at each of the options available. Have patience; if you learn how to control Photoshop's brushes now, your productivity and creativity will be increased dramatically as you create your paintings.

Remember that, for the most part, you may want to use only one or two brushes for any given painting. Sometimes you will use a few more brushes, but almost never will you want to use everything that is at your disposal. To be able to make those decisions you need to know

- Where Photoshop's brushes are located and how to access them
- How to change the basic properties of a brush
- The brush options available to you in the Brushes palette

Where Are the Photoshop Brushes?

While this may seem obvious, there may be a few of you who don't know where the brushes are located. Never fear; they are easy to find. Figure 13.1 shows the location of the Brush tool in Photoshop.

FIGURE 13.1   The location of the Brush tool in Photoshop.

The Brush tool is the eighth icon on the toolbar if you are using a toolbar that is a single icon wide. If your toolbar is two icons wide, the Brush tool is the fourth icon down on the right side of the toolbar. If you click this icon and hold down your mouse button, the icon will expand to show the Pencil tool and the Color Replacement tool. Figure 13.2 shows the Pencil and Color Replacement tools.

FIGURE 13.2   The submenu item showing the Brush tool, the Pencil tool, and the Color Replacement Tool.

The Pencil tool is a very small version of the brush. You can increase its size, but you should have no reason to do so. Leave the Pencil tool small for fine work and use the Brush tool for painting. The Color Replacement tool will replace a selected color in your image with a new color. The keyboard shortcut is "B" for all three tools.

When you click the Brush icon, notice that the Options bar at the top of the screen changes to reflect the currently selected tool, as shown in Figure 13.3.

The first icon on the Options bar is the Tool Preset Picker. When the Brush tool is selected and the Preset Picker activated, Photoshop displays three brushes by default. This is a great place to add and store your most commonly used brushes to have them close for easy access. Figure 13.4 shows the Tool Preset Picker menu.

Depending on how you have customized the Photoshop CS3 workspace, you may or may not have a Tool Preset icon visible. In my current layout the Tool Presets icon is located at the top of the icon buttons in the upper-right corner of my workspace (Figure 13.5).

FIGURE 13.3 The Brush Options bar.

FIGURE 13.4 The Tool Preset Picker menu.

FIGURE 13.5 The Tool Presets icon.

It stores your most commonly used brushes along with any other frequently used tools you may care to add. The icon can be expanded simply by clicking on it, or it can be dragged off to display the tools located within it (Figure 13.6).

FIGURE 13.6　The Tool Presets fly out palette docked and the Tool Presets fly out palette undocked.

The next icon on the Options bar is the Brush Picker (Figure 13.7).

FIGURE 13.7　The Brush Picker with Brush Diameter and Brush Hardness highlighted.

Click this icon and you will be presented with a visual display of all your currently loaded brushes. The default selection is large and presents you with more than enough brushes to paint almost anything with. You will also notice two controls that are available when this palette is open: Brush Diameter and Brush Hardness (indicated by red arrows).

How to Change Brush Properties

You have a number of options for previewing what your brush looks like. The default display, shown in Figure 13.7, shows a small icon of the brush profile and what a typical stroke will look like. Sometimes you may want to switch to a larger display of the brush profile. You access the control panel for the Brush Picker by clicking on the small triangle within the circle on the right side of the picker. Clicking on the triangle will give you a number of options for displaying your brushes along with available brush libraries you can load. Figure 13.8 shows the Brush Picker with the large thumbnail option selected within the control panel.

FIGURE 13.8   The Brush Picker with large thumbnails of the brush profiles displayed.

The third item on the Options bar is the mode selector (Figure 13.9).

FIGURE 13.9   The Brush Mode menu.

These modes are similar to the modes that you can apply to individual layers. You must remember, though, that unlike layers that can be deleted, changed, and manipulated, brush modes are permanent in comparison. Behind and Clear may be grayed out in the menu. This is because these modes do not work on the background layer if it is selected. Refer to the Photoshop manual for a more in-depth discussion of the modes.

The next menu item on the Options bar is Opacity. This option is self-explanatory; it lets you specify how opaque or transparent individual pixels will appear when you are painting. Figure 13.10 shows the same brush using various opacities for its strokes.

When you decrease the opacity of the stroke, you are able to see the underlying strokes. You can alter the opacity of the stroke by using the slider under the Opacity setting, by entering a numerical value, or holding the Shift key and a number key.

The next-to-last item on the Options bar is Flow. Flow visually looks fairly similar to Opacity, but it isn't the same. The Flow slider determines how quickly and evenly your digital paint is applied. When you use a high setting, the pixels are filled in quickly and very closely spaced together. As you gradually reduce the flow, the pixels are not filled in as quickly or as evenly. You can see the results of gradually reducing the flow in Figure 13.11.

FIGURE 13.10   The Brush Opacity slider along with an image showing strokes using various opacity settings.

FIGURE 13.11   The Flow slider and an image showing strokes using different flow settings.

As with the opacity, you can change the amount of flow by moving the slider, entering a value, or tapping one of the number keys.

The final item on the Options bar is the Airbrush icon, shown in Figure 13.12.

FIGURE 13.12   The Airbrush icon.

Clicking and holding this icon will cause digital paint to be deposited as long as you hold your stylus pressed to the tablet. It will do the same if you are painting with the mouse and hold down the left mouse button.

Moving across the Options bar you are able to pick a brush preset using the Toggle the Brushes Palette button (Figure 13.13).

This button brings up the Brushes palette and displays all the currently loaded brushes. Using any preset, you can paint in any of a number of different modes selected from the drop-down list. Once you have selected the brush profile and mode, you can then change either the brush opacity or brush flow, or both. Finally, by clicking the Airbrush icon, you can determine if the brush will continuously deposit paint while holding down either the left mouse button or your stylus.

It is also worth noting that you can change the default size and opacity of your brushes using keyboard shortcuts. Using keyboard shortcuts can dramatically increase your speed when painting. Consult your Photoshop documentation for the specific shortcut keys for the brushes.

FIGURE 13.13   The Toggle the Brushes palette button.

That's about it for our simple explanation of how to pick a brush and change a few of the brush settings using the Options bar. In the next section, we will dig deeper into the workings of the more advanced brush controls available in Photoshop.

SECTION 2: THE PHOTOSHOP BRUSHES PALETTE

While the Options bar gives you some control over how your brush will behave, the Brushes palette is where the fun really begins. Using this palette, you can control virtually any aspect of how your brush acts.

Depending on your custom layout, the Brushes palette is one of the icons located in the upper-right corner of your screen (Figure 13.14).

Click on the icon and let's look at what is revealed. This palette will stay visible until you click the icon again. Drag off the Brushes palette to keep it visible all the time. You can also quickly access the Brushes palette by clicking the Toggle the Brushes palette icon located on the far right of the Options bar.

The Brushes palette can look daunting when opened, as you can see in Figure 13.15.

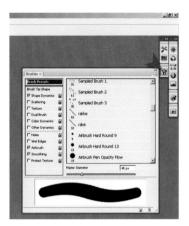

FIGURE 13.14   The Brushes icon.

FIGURE 13.15   The Brushes palette.

So many controls are available that deciding where to start can be overwhelming. Should you begin with the Shape Dynamic controls? The Scattering controls? Texture? Dual Brush? Color Dynamics? There are just too many options!

To make things as simple as possible, let's start at the top and work our way down the palette settings. The first thing to notice is the far-left edge of the palette. Here you will see a number of small boxes. These boxes will either be checked or not checked, depending on the brush that you currently have selected. A check means that the option is currently active for the brush you are using. Clicking on the small padlock icon locks those options for the current brush. These boxes and icons are highlighted with red arrows in Figure 13.16.

FIGURE 13.16 The option boxes and padlock icons located in the Brushes palette.

The first two options are different in that they do not have a small check box to their left. This may cause you to overlook these first and very basic controls, the Brush Presets and the Brush Tip Shape.

Brush Presets

The Brush Presets are self-explanatory; they simply display the brushes that are currently loaded in Photoshop, as shown in Figure 13.17.

FIGURE 13.17 The Brush Presets located in the Brushes palette.

Brush Tip Shape

Click on the Brush Tip Shape option, and you get the palette shown in Figure 13.18.

FIGURE 13.18   The Brush Tip Shape
menu located in the Brushes palette.

In this first palette, you set some of the very basic parameters of the brush you
will be creating or using. This palette displays the brush tips that Photoshop currently has loaded. Within the default brushes, you will notice brushes ranging from
simple round brushes to leaf shapes. Also displayed at the bottom of the palette is a
preview of your currently selected brush that reflects the current brush settings. You
can change brush tips by clicking any of the small icons showing the brush profile. If
you are simply going to change the brush you are currently using, do not click any
of these different brush tips.

To show how some of the other controls function within this palette, select the
hard elliptical 45 brush, as shown in Figure 13.19.

FIGURE 13.19   Selecting the hard
elliptical 45 brush.

Right under the brush tip display you will notice the first control: the Diameter
slider. You will also see a box showing the current diameter of the brush tip. You can
move this slider up or down to change the diameter of the brush tip and display an

update of what the brush will look like in the preview window at the bottom of the palette. You can also click your cursor in the box and enter a numerical value for the diameter if you wish. Below are two small boxes called *flip x* and *flip y*. Checking one of these boxes will flip the brush on either its x- or y-axis; if you check both, Photoshop will flip the brush on both axes. The larger display to the right (showing an ellipse with an arrow aligned along its major axis and two dots aligned on the shorter axis) contains the Angle and Roundness controls. There are also two boxes labeled Angle and Roundness; they display the current angle that the brush is aligned to and how round the brush is. In our current brush, the angle alignment is 45° to the right with a roundness of 45% of a circle. You can change these values either by entering numeric values in the boxes or by using the displayed ellipse. To change the angle, click and drag on the major axis displayed as the arrow. To change the roundness, click and drag on one of the two dots on the minor axis. Figure 13.20 shows the Angle and Roundness controls.

FIGURE 13.20 The Angle and Roundness controls.

The next slider below the Angle and Roundness controls is the Hardness slider, with a range from 0% to 100%. At the 100% setting, you can see that the edges of the brush displayed in the preview are very crisp (Figure 13.21).

If you drag the slider down to the left or enter a different numeric value, you will see how the edge grows progressively softer in the brush preview window (Figure 13.22).

The final control in this portion of the brush settings palette is the Spacing control. This consists of a slider and a check box and determines how closely together Photoshop will put the individual brush dabs. Currently, the check box is selected, and the preview window shows your brush stroke with very smooth and close spacing, as shown in Figure 13.23.

FIGURE 13.21   The Hardness slider
and brush preview window.

FIGURE 13.22   Moving the Hardness
slider down gives a softer stroke.

FIGURE 13.23   The Spacing control
slider.

Now notice what happens when you move the Spacing slider up to a higher value. You begin to see more and more space between the brush dabs until you can actually see the individual dabs, as shown in Figure 13.24.

FIGURE 13.24   Moving the slider up on the Spacing control puts increasing amounts of space between paint dabs.

Unchecking the Spacing box takes away the control you have over the dab spacing and will give you a random result (Figure 13.25) unless you have a steady hand.

FIGURE 13.25   Random spacing in the brush stroke caused by deselecting the Spacing box.

The stroke where the dabs appear closer together is made by moving the stylus very slowly; moving the stylus quickly results in more space between the dabs.

Shape Dynamics

The next option is called Shape Dynamics. Click on this menu item to open the palette shown in Figure 13.26.

FIGURE 13.26   The Shape Dynamics palette.

Deselect the Shape Dynamics box and notice what happens to your stroke in the preview window (Figure 13.27).

FIGURE 13.27   Deselecting the Shape Dynamics options and the results.

Along with showing a stroke that now has very little size variation within it, Photoshop grays out all of the menu options.

Now check the Shape Dynamics box to activate the Shape Dynamics palette. Within this palette, you will find six controls. The first slider at the top of the palette is Size Jitter, with a box immediately below giving you a menu that lets you control the effect. Move the small arrow to the right and notice what happens within the preview window. The size of the individual brush dabs begins to vary, and the stroke looks rougher and more random, as shown in Figure 13.28.

FIGURE 13.28 Deselecting the Shape Dynamics options and the results.

The next control is the Minimum Diameter slider, shown in Figure 13.29. This slider set to a low value will make the brush dabs very small at the beginning of a stroke. Move the slider up, and the beginning dabs will get progressively larger. At the maximum setting, there will be no variation of size within the stroke.

FIGURE 13.29 The Minimum Diameter slider.

Angle Jitter is the next control. Most of these controls are self-explanatory, and this one is no exception. With the Angle Jitter set to 0%, as shown in Figure 13.30, the angles of the brush dabs remain for the most part identical. Move the slider up or enter a numeric value, and the angle of the brush dabs begins to vary, as shown in Figure 13.31.

FIGURE 13.30   The Angle Jitter set to 0%.

FIGURE 13.31   Increasing the Angle Jitter slider.

The brush dab spacing has been increased to show the effect more clearly. Once again you can pick the control method for the effect.

The next control is Roundness Jitter, shown in Figure 13.32.

This control will vary the roundness of the brush dabs as you paint. As you raise the value by typing in a value or moving the slider, you can see the results in the preview window. The roundness of the dabs varies from very thin to round. You can use the Roundness Jitter control in conjunction with the Minimum Roundness slider. Setting the slider low will make the dabs very thin, and higher values will make the dabs rounder.

FIGURE 13.32 The Roundness Jitter slider.

Scattering

Check the Scattering box to activate the Scattering palette, shown in Figure 13.33. This control does exactly what it says: it scatters the brush dabs within the brush stroke. The more the slider is moved to the right, the more the individual dabs will be offset from the stroke of the stylus. Check the Both Axes box, and the dabs will be scattered in a more random fashion along both axes. Eventually, if the scatter is set high enough, the direction of the original stroke can virtually disappear, as Figure 13.34 shows.

FIGURE 13.33 The Scattering palette lets you "scatter" the brush dabs.

Below the Scatter slider are two additional sliders. The first is Count, and it does just what the name implies. From the lowest value of 1 to the maximum value of 100, as you move the slider to the right, you increase the number of dabs that will be scattered. Below the Count slider is the Count Jitter slider, with a control box below the slider (Figure 13.35).

FIGURE 13.34   A stroke with a very high Scatter setting.

FIGURE 13.35   The Count Jitter slider and menu for picking what will drive the effect.

The control box sets what drives the effect. To see the results most clearly, set the control to Fade and move the Count Jitter slider all the way to the right. You will notice that a higher amount of jittery dabs begin at the start of the stroke and "fade" as the stroke moves to the right. Experiment with additional settings to see the result.

Texture

The next series of controls are in the Texture palette (Figure 13.36). Checking the Texture box will mix the currently selected pattern with your brush stroke. You can select a different pattern within the Texture palette by clicking the pattern's thumbnail. You can also invert the pattern and see how it reacts by checking the small box just to the right of the pattern thumbnail.

FIGURE 13.36   The Texture palette showing a selected pattern and its effect on the brush stroke.

Below the preview image is a slider that you can use to vary the scale of the selected pattern. You will also notice the mode selector, where you can select how the pattern will interact with the brush stroke. These modes are similar to the layer modes you are familiar with. The Depth slider determines how much of the pattern will interact with the stroke. A low value means that very little of the pattern will interact, while a higher value means that more of the pattern will be visible within your stroke. You can also enter a numeric value in the box above the slider. The two remaining sliders are available only if you have the Texture Each Tip box checked right above the mode selector. Figure 13.37 shows the results of adding Depth and Depth Jitter to a brush.

FIGURE 13.37   The Texture palette showing the results of adding Depth and Depth Jitter to a brush.

These controls obviously work best if you have a brush with multiple tips. Experiment with the sliders at different settings to get a variety of nice, rough brush strokes.

Dual Brush

Moving down, we come to the Dual Brush palette, which makes it possible for you to blend two different brushes together. When you open this palette, notice that you are presented with the currently loaded brush presets (Figure 13.38).

FIGURE 13.38   The Dual Brush palette.

This blending of the brushes' options will work best with two very different brush types, so pick accordingly. Usually a very large and fat brush will work well with a brush with higher scatter settings. Picking the mode of the blend will also have a great effect on the look of the brush. The Diameter, Spacing, Scatter, and Count sliders all affect the chosen brush as they do in the other palettes.

Color Dynamics

When you're painting in Photoshop, the color of the brush is whatever you've set the primary color to. The Color Dynamics palette (Figure 13.39) makes it possible to vary the colors used in your brush. To demonstrate how this works, set the background color to a color of your choice and move the Foreground/Background Jitter slider up to 100%. Leave the default control set to Brush Pressure.

Notice that in the preview window nothing has seemed to change. Unfortunately, the preview window does not display the changes in the brush when you change the settings in the Color Dynamics palette. To see the changes you have made to your brush, you will need to make a stroke in your painting or, better yet, in a test image. Figure 13.40 shows an image with a stroke using the settings in Figure 13.39.

FIGURE 13.39 The Color Dynamics palette.

FIGURE 13.40 The result of increasing the Foreground/Background Jitter slider.

What is happening here? Assuming that you chose any color other than white for your background color, shouldn't you be getting a stroke that displays variations between the foreground and background colors and not between black and white? For the user new to the brushes controls, this can be confusing. There is one more slider that must be moved for you to get jitter between the foreground and background colors, and that is the Purity slider. Right now the slider is set to a value of −100. At this setting there is absolutely no pure color in your stroke. Read this as no color at all, just variations of black and white. Move the slider to 0, as shown in Figure 13.41.

FIGURE 13.41   Increasing the Purity slider.

Notice that the preview window does not change. It never will. You need to once again make a stroke in your test image. Now you should notice that the color of the stroke does indeed vary between the foreground and background colors, as Figure 13.42 shows.

FIGURE 13.42   The result of moving the Purity slider.

If the Purity setting of 0 gives you the jitter between the foreground and background colors, what does increasing the Purity setting to a greater value yield? Increasing the Purity value increases the intensity of the color. This increase makes the jitter greater so that it is no longer just between the foreground and background colors but between the foreground and a very intense background variation. Be careful not to raise the Purity setting above 0 if you want to vary only between the foreground and background colors; Figure 13.43 shows what happens when you set it too high.

FIGURE 13.43   The resulting stroke when the Purity slider is set too high.

Assuming that you now have your brush set to jitter between the foreground and background colors as you want, you can explore the other sliders. They are, for the most part, self-explanatory, as you can see in Figure 13.44.

FIGURE 13.44   The remaining sliders in the Color Dynamics palette.

- The Hue Jitter slider will change the hue (color) of the background color that the brush jitters to. With a low setting, the hue will vary only slightly away from the background color. An extremely high setting will vary hue jitter to a color completely different from the original background color.

- The Saturation Jitter slider will vary the saturation (grayness) of the background color.
- The Brightness Jitter slider will vary the brightness (value) of the background color.

Once again, to see the results of varying these sliders, you will need to try out your strokes in a test image, as the preview window does not display the color information.

Other Dynamics

The Other Dynamics palette features controls for two settings we've already discussed. Recall the Opacity and Flow controls in the Options bar that appear when you pick the Brush tool. While these controls adjust the flow and opacity for the stroke overall, the settings in the Other Dynamics palette (Figure 13.45) set the flow and opacity on a dab-by-dab level.

FIGURE 13.45   The Other Dynamics palette showing the Opacity and Flow sliders.

Because these settings work on the individual dab in the stroke, they can be used in conjunction with the general Opacity and Flow settings in the Options bar to create almost limitless varieties of effects.

The last five menu items in the Brushes palette (Figure 13.46) do not open their own sub-palettes. Instead, these items are just boxes that can be checked or unchecked as you like. What follows is a description of what each of the check boxes does.

Noise: Checking the Noise box will add a grainy effect to the brush stroke, as Figure 13.47 shows. The effect is most noticeable if the hardness of your stroke is very low.

FIGURE 13.46   The last five menu items in the Brushes palette.

FIGURE 13.47   The results of checking the Noise box.

Wet Edges: Checking the Wet Edges box will give you a puddling effect. This in some respects resembles the nonuniform way that watercolor will sometimes dry, as shown in Figure 13.48.

Airbrush: This check box, when selected, does the same thing as the Airbrush icon on the Brush Options bar.

Smoothing: When the Smoothing option is checked, Photoshop will "smooth" a stroke made by a brush (Figure 13.49). With Smoothing unchecked, a brush will sometimes draw small, straight areas when painting a stroke. Notice the arrow pointing to the slight angle visible on the curve with Smoothing unchecked. If you look closely, you can see several slight angles within the stroke.

FIGURE 13.48   The puddling effect caused by checking the Wet Edges box.

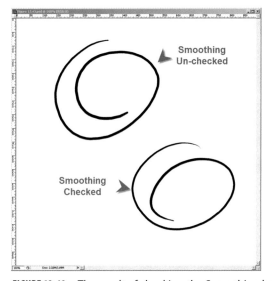

FIGURE 13.49   The result of checking the Smoothing box.

Protect Texture: This last check box works only with textured brushes, and you will see no change in any of the other brushes. When checked, the option applies the same pattern at the same scale to all brushes that paint with a texture. This makes it easy to have a consistent look throughout a painting that uses patterns.

In this chapter we have explored the Brushes palette and have seen the innumerable ways that the default brushes can be altered to suit your particular needs. This is basic to your understanding of painting within Photoshop. You must know your tool and how to make it behave the way you expect and want. In the following section, we will look at the process of making your own custom brushes and not just altering settings of the default libraries.

SECTION 3: CREATING YOUR OWN PHOTOSHOP BRUSHES

Why with all the brushes that already ship with Photoshop would anyone want to create their own brushes? The answer to this question is simple. You save custom brushes to do exactly what you want when you want to do it. You could, if you had the time and inclination, re-create a brush or create an entirely new brush every time you painted, but this would indeed be a lengthy and time-consuming way of working. Or suppose you are commissioned to do a series of images that all need to look and feel similar. Being able to create and save libraries and variants of brushes makes this possible. Fortunately, in Photoshop you do have the ability to create and save brushes and brush libraries. You can create an entire custom set for every project you work on if you care to. In this section, we look at creating and organizing your brushes.

Creating and Saving Brushes in Photoshop

You already have learned how to change the settings of the default brushes to get them to behave like you want by using the brush options. Suppose there is one custom brush that you keep coming back to time and time again. Here is how to save your new brush to the Tools Preset menu.

Click on the Brush Preset Picker icon located on the left of the Tool Options bar. From the menu that opens, click on the small triangle and three bars on the top left of the palette (Figure 13.50).

FIGURE 13.50   Click the small triangle and three bars on the Brush Preset Picker.

This displays a menu loaded with different commands. The second command is New Brush Preset (Figure 13.51).

FIGURE 13.51   The New Brush Preset command.

Click this command and a dialog box opens asking you to name your new brush, as shown in Figure 13.52.

FIGURE 13.52   The Save Brush dialog box.

Name your brush and click OK. Your newly saved brush now appears at the bottom of the entire list of brushes. It is as simple as that. There is even a small shortcut you can use if you want, and this is displayed at the bottom of the Brush palette. Click on the small button next to the trashcan at the bottom of the palette (Figure 13.53). This immediately opens the dialog box where you can name your brush and save it.

FIGURE 13.53 The small button that opens the Save Brush dialog box.

You may have noticed that a lot of additional items on the menu are displayed by clicking on the triangle on the Brush Preset Picker (Figure 13.51). For the most part, these commands are self-explanatory, but let's go over them quickly here.

Below the New Brush Preset command are three commands, Clear Brush Controls, Reset All Locked Settings, and Copy Texture to Other Tools. The first two commands set all the settings of a custom brush back to a default state. Copy Texture to Other Tools does just what it says.

The next two commands, Rename Brush and Delete Brush, do just what they say: rename or delete brushes in the preset list.

The next six commands change the way the brushes are displayed in the Brush Preset picker. The best way to see what they do is to click on them and see what changes.

The next command opens the Preset Manager. Here you can arrange, name, delete, and perform a number of different operations on your brush libraries.

The next four commands do the following. the Reset Brushes command resets the brushes in Photoshop back to the default library and settings. Load Brushes allows you to load additional or custom brush libraries. Save Brushes lets you save all of the currently loaded brushes into a custom library, and Replace Brushes replaces the currently loaded library with a different one. Below those commands, you will see a list of brush libraries currently available to Photoshop.

Creating a Custom Brush in Photoshop Using a Photographic Texture

There is another way to create brushes in Photoshop that involves more than just tweaking default brushes. This method involves using images to create an almost endless supply of custom brushes. You can make brushes from photos or scanned images, or you can even draw your own.

This method of creating brushes is unbelievably simple and straightforward. In this section, we will create a brush from a photographic image, though you can use the same procedure for creating a brush from a drawing or anything else you can bring up in Photoshop.

ON THE CD

Generally, you should look for imagery that has good contrasts between the lights and darks. For this example, this photo of a rather strange rock formation makes the perfect subject (Figure 13.54). The image is included on the CD-ROM.

FIGURE 13.54   A photo of a strange rock formation that is perfect for creating a custom brush.

While it is possible to make a brush as large as you want, for practical painting purposes, it is probably best to stick with a brush that is around 600 pixels in size or smaller. With the photo of the rock formation opened in Photoshop, resize the image so that the size of the image is 600 pixels in both dimensions, as shown in Figure 13.55.

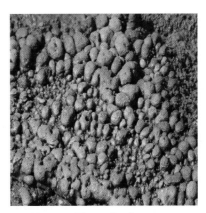

FIGURE 13.55   The resized texture.

Though you can save a brush that is a combination of any width and height, square-based brushes seem to work very well. Increase the contrast somewhat and convert the image to grayscale, as shown in Figure 13.56.

FIGURE 13.56   The image converted to grayscale, with contrast increased.

At this point, you can, if you want, create a brush from this image. Actually, you can create a brush at any step in the process that suits you. To create the brush, you simply go into the Edit menu and select Define Brush Preset, as shown in Figure 13.57.

Your new brush is displayed as a thumbnail in the Brush Name dialog box, shown in Figure 13.58.

FIGURE 13.57   The Define Brush Preset command.

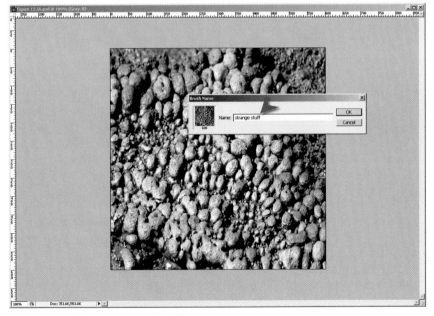

FIGURE 13.58   Name your new brush.

Name the brush anything that you would like and click OK. You now have a new brush. The brush is at its rough state at this point. Now it is up to you to go into the brush options and tweak the brush to get it to behave just as you want.

While these steps will provide you with a perfectly usable brush, just the addition of a few more steps will give you a better and more customizable brush, so to continue, do the following. Once you have converted the image to grayscale and adjusted the contrast, to give you an idea of how the brush will look when painting, add an alpha channel under the Channels tab. It does not matter what you call the alpha; the default of "Alpha 1" is just fine.

With the alpha channel active, pick the Gradient Fill tool and fill with a radial gradient using black and white, as shown in Figure 13.59.

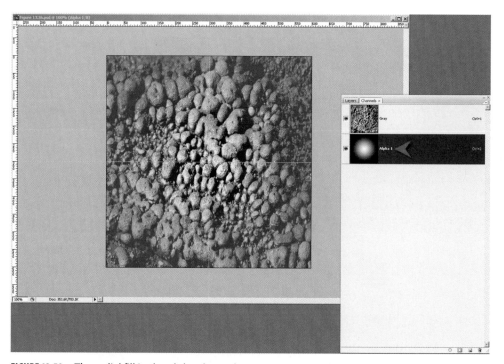

FIGURE 13.59 The radial fill in the alpha channel.

Make the original layer active and load the alpha channel as a selection. You should see marching ants around the middle of the image, as shown in Figure 13.60.

You can see what the marching ants look like very lightly against the image. Copy and paste back into the image. Hide the background layer, and you will have something that looks like Figure 13.61.

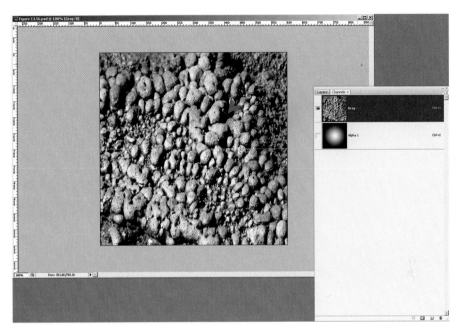

FIGURE 13.60   The alpha channel loaded as a selection.

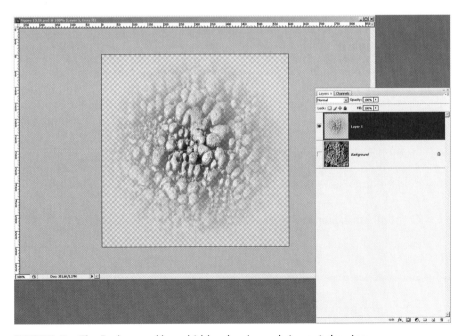

FIGURE 13.61   The Background layer hidden, leaving only Layer 1 showing.

Now you have a nice image that fades to transparent on the edges. Go ahead and tweak the contrast if you like. Once again, go to the Edit menu and select the Define Brush Preset command. Name your paper something descriptive and click Yes (Figure 13.62).

FIGURE 13.62   Saving your new brush.

ON THE CD

The previous method will work with any image. With experimentation, you will find a working method that suits your painting style best. Many rough brush libraries are included on the CD-ROM and were created using this procedure.

Now that you have created a number of different brushes, it is time to learn what to do with them. The next section describes how to save and create brush libraries. Use the following instructions, and you will soon have a vast number of organized brush libraries that you can share with anyone who uses Photoshop.

Creating Brush Libraries of Your Custom Brushes

Assuming that you have created a number of new brushes and saved them, there is one last thing that you will want to do: create a library of your new brushes. The reason that you would want to do this is simple. Should you ever by accident (or intentionally) reset your brushes back to their default setting, if you have not saved all your custom brushes into another library, they will be lost.

It is very simple to save your own brushes, and you should do it regularly. Just select the Save Brushes command from the Brush Presets menu, as shown in Figure 13.63.

FIGURE 13.63   The Save Brushes command.

This opens a dialog box asking you what to call your new library and gives you the chance to save your library to any location on your computer, as shown in Figure 13.64.

FIGURE 13.64   Saving a brush library.

It is easiest to save to the default location so Photoshop always knows where to find your new brushes. Once you have saved your new brush library, you will want to open the Preset Manager (Figure 13.65). Here you can delete any brushes you may not want, rename, and click and drag the brush icons to rearrange the brushes.

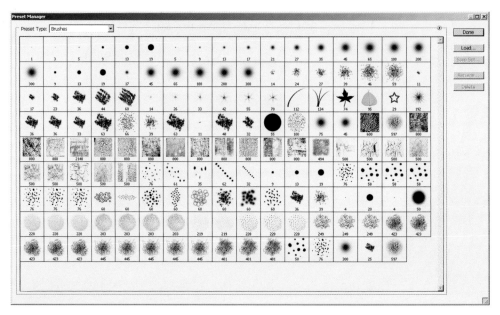

FIGURE 13.65   The Brush Preset Manager.

Several very good books can take you deeper into Photoshop's brushes if you care to find out more information, but these few and simple steps will fill most all of your brush needs.

In this section, you have learned about Photoshop's powerful brush engine. You have learned how to tweak the default brushes to get them to behave for your particular painting style, how to create custom brushes from images, how to save brushes, and how to organize them into your own personal libraries. Beware that sometimes creating new and innovative brushes becomes almost as much fun as the actual painting.

CONCLUSION

Now we move on to Part III of our book: tutorials covering different subject matter. The first tutorial will cover painting eyes. After all, in a book on character design and digital painting, what better place to start than with the windows to the soul.

DIGITAL PAINTING: BRINGING IT ALL TOGETHER IN PHOTOSHOP CS3

Two different versions of Photoshop CS3 are available: Photoshop CS3 and Photoshop CS3 Extended. The version that you choose will ultimately depend on the type of work that you do. CS3 Extended offers extra features for some specialized tasks. CS3 is also significantly more expensive than the regular version. Generally speaking, the features that are useful for digital 2D painting are included in both Photoshop CS3 and Photoshop CS3 Extended, and these features are the ones that will be covered in the following tutorials.

Some features in Photoshop CS3 are worth mentioning even though they are not directly involved in the painting or image creation process. The first and most noticeable new feature is the new interface. On the options bar, you will notice a drop-down menu named Workspace (Figure III.1).

Here are eight standard options for your Photoshop workspace based on the type of work you intend to do. There is one for Painting and Retouching. This is a good workspace to start with for digital painting, and you can adjust the menus and palettes to meet your particular way of working. Notice that the palettes collapse to icons with the click of the mouse button (Figure III.2).

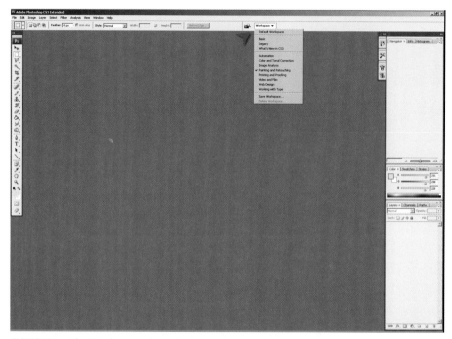

FIGURE III.1 The Workspace drop-down menu.

FIGURE III.2 Collapsing the workspace palettes to icons.

You can decide if you want the name of the palette to be displayed along with the associated icon (Figure III.3).

FIGURE III.3   The collapsed palettes with some showing only the icon representation and others showing the palette name along with the associated icon.

Individual icons will also expand into a palette with another click (Figure III.4).

When you have your ideal workspace, you can save it and recall it at any time as you switch between different workspaces to suit your tasks.

These additional features are new and valuable to the digital painter:

- Quick Selection tool
- Refine Edge feature of the quick selection tool
- Vanishing Point tool
- Non-destructive smart filters
- New black and white conversion features
- Improved Curves

This section contains tutorials on how to approach painting different subject matter. By no means do these tutorials show the only or even the best way of approaching these subjects. They show only one way that I use to approach the subject. This book is about character design and painting, so the majority of the tutorials and demonstrations in this section are of organic subject matter.

FIGURE III.4 Individual icons will expand into a palette with a click of the stylus on the icon.

In Part III, the following assumptions have been made:

You already have a basic working knowledge of Photoshop. When we talk about different commands and effects, it is assumed that you know what we are talking about. In addition, most chapters in Part III have a little section called "What You Need to Know About Photoshop for This Chapter" that further outlines what you are expected to know.

You, the reader and artist, should do your own interpretation of the steps taken here. It would be preferable for you to experiment as you are following along.

At this point in the book, you need more graphics and less explanation. The chapters in this section are very heavy on graphics and lighter on text than the beginning demonstrations. Most artists would rather look at step-by-step images with brief explanations as opposed to long-winded paragraphs that attempt to explain a visual concept. After all, isn't one picture worth a thousand words?

You will notice in these demonstrations that the author often changes his mind about what he's doing, which is both a fault and a blessing. A firm idea almost always comes to mind, but then often something not previously considered pops up, changing the direction of the work.

If a custom texture or brush has not been mentioned before in the book and is used for the first time in this section, it will be included in the relevant chapter's folder on the CD-ROM.

Photoshop has been used for all images. Much of what you see here is also applicable to other programs, but if you use Photoshop, it will be easier for you to duplicate the steps.

PAINTING AN EYE

This chapter covers one of the basic skills needed when you are painting characters: painting a realistic eye. Painting the features of a face is not as hard as it sometimes seems. In this chapter, you will learn a simple way to paint a human eye. This method, as with most of the demonstrations in this book, is applicable to just about any type of eye that you may need to paint.

WHAT YOU NEED TO KNOW ABOUT PHOTOSHOP FOR THIS CHAPTER

This tutorial assumes that you know some fundamentals of working in Photoshop, such as:

- Where individual palettes are located. In this particular tutorial, we will not be changing very many of Photoshop's defaults.
- How to adjust a brush's opacity.
- How to resize your brush and sample color from within the image (using hot keys).

You can arrange Photoshop's workspace to suit your own liking, so this chapter does not discuss where to locate specific items.

Once again, always remember when you are painting on the computer to save your files. Make it a habit to save numerically named versions of your work. One of the best things about digital painting is this ability to save multiple versions that you can revert to if you make a major mistake.

| TUTORIAL 14.1 | **PAINTING THE WINDOW INTO A CHARACTER'S SOUL, THE EYE** |

In this tutorial, we aren't doing any preliminary drawing or scanning sketches; however, if doing so makes you more comfortable, feel free to scan in a sketch or drawing that you have done. To paint an eye, follow these steps:

1. Start Photoshop and create a new image document (600 × 600 pixels is a good size). Make sure that the white of the image is covered. Either create the image with a colored paper or fill the canvas with a light-gray color.
2. Select the Airbrush Pen Opacity Flow brush. (This brush is a default Photoshop brush; if you do not see it in your Brushes palette, reset your brushes.)
3. You need to make one change to the default brush before you begin drawing your eye. In the Brush Tip Shape palette, change the hardness to about 50%, as shown in Figure 14.5. By changing these settings, you create a brush that looks slightly softer along the edges as you draw. This brush also tends to produce a softer gray if you press lightly on your stylus and becomes darker as you press harder. This is a great way to work because your initial strokes are light, and as you refine your drawing, you can press harder to make the strokes darker.

FIGURE 14.5   Brush settings for drawing the eye.

4. Set your brush's color to a mid-value gray, set the opacity to about 30% and the size to around 10, and then begin drawing an eye. As you draw, remember that the eye is basically spherical in shape and is surrounded by the fleshy folds of the eyelids. While drawing, you must always remember the 3D aspects of your subject, or your images will look flat and lifeless. Your initial sketch should look something like Figure 14.6.

FIGURE 14.6   Your initial sketch of the eye should look something like this.

5. Let's add a little color to the sketch. From the Filters menu, choose Render, and then click Lighting Effects. Add an omni light right about the iris of the eye. Change the color of the light to some nice fleshy color. Move the Brightness slider down so that all the color is not washed out to white (Figure 14.7).

FIGURE 14.7 The Lighting Effects menu showing the Omni Light and the color of the light adjusted to a fleshy color.

6. Once you apply the lighting effect, your image should look something like Figure 14.8.

FIGURE 14.8 The lighting effect applied to the sketch of the eye.

7. Switch to the Airbrush Soft Round brush. Set the Opacity slider to a fairly low value of between 20% and 40%. From the Color palette, select a dark orange color to represent the dark flesh color and begin painting in the shadow areas of the eye, as shown in Figure 14.9. Do not worry about "staying in the lines"; just concentrate on getting color down. Do not paint too opaquely or you will lose your underlying image. Switch back to your original brush and paint in some of the iris's color. Notice that the colors used in Figure 14.9 are not intense. A painting of uniform, bright intensity is very tiring on the eye.

FIGURE 14.9   Painting in the shadow areas and the iris's color.

8. Select your original brush again if you have changed back and forth to the Airbrush and start redrawing any of the eye that was painted over too opaquely. Begin to add in more detail and additional color, as shown in Figure 14.10.

FIGURE 14.10   Redrawing the eye over the airbrushed colors.

9. Start to work some lighter and brighter color into the image. Notice in Figure 14.11 that as the eye is painted, deep reds and subtle pinks have been put in the corners and lower lids, that the blue color of the iris is not intense, and that the white of the eye is anything but white. Also notice the amount of red that is in the deepest shadow areas. Try to use deep reds instead of blacks when drawing the darkest areas. Black will kill the life of the image, whereas deep red will add life to it. Do not worry that the strokes are looking rough at this point.

FIGURE 14.11   Working lighter and brighter colors into the eye painting.

10. Continue to add more color. Do not get too intense, but do get brighter. In Figure 14.12, some greens and browns have been added to the iris for variety, the white of the eye has been lightened, and some lighter flesh tones have been added around the eye. Also notice that highlights are being added. Because an eye's surface is wet, the highlights are very sharp and shiny. The edges need to be relatively crisp and lean slightly toward the color of the light source. All of this work is done using the original brush while varying the size and opacity where needed.

11. By now, your eye looks pretty good, though it is somewhat messy. Let's clean it up a little. Use the blending method described in Chapter 11 and begin to smooth out some of the rough strokes. Remember that you are not trying to obliterate the strokes but simply soften them a touch. The last thing to do is add back some of the detail that has been blended out. Switch back to your original brush and redraw some of the small detail in the creases and lids of the eyes that may have been lost in the blending process, add a few eyelashes, paint the eyebrow, paint a few of the small veins in the corner of the eye, and you are done, as shown in Figure 14.13.

FIGURE 14.12　Adding more color to the iris of the eye.

FIGURE 14.13　Slight blending and reestablishing the detail to finish the eye.

CONCLUSION

Well, that is about all there is to painting an eye. You can use this general technique when painting virtually any eye on any character. Put a lot of time and practice into painting eyes. They are one of the most important features in a face and the one that grabs most of our attention when we are interacting with each other. In the next chapter, we will expand on what we have learned and concentrate on painting the entire face.

PAINTING A FACE

face may be one of the most difficult subject matters that an artist tackles. In this chapter, we will paint a human face. The techniques presented here are pretty much applicable to painting any sort of face, be it human or alien.

TUTORIAL 15.1	**GENERAL WORKING METHODS YOU MAY WANT TO USE WHEN PAINTING A FACE**

Here is one method you can use to realize a full-color, digitally painted face and head. Just follow these steps:

1. Start by making a sketch, as shown in Figure 15.1. You can draw it by using either the traditional paper-and-pencil method or drawing directly on the computer; it really does not matter. If you start with a pencil sketch, you will, of course, need to scan the image into your computer. At this stage, you should consider resolution issues, along with what the final output will be. Will your image be used for print or on the Web? A print image will need to be at a much higher resolution than a Web image. When starting with the scan, consider working with an image that has a resolution of 200 dpi and that is grayscale. A 200-dpi resolution is large enough to let you include all the necessary facial details, is a high enough resolution to print well, and is small enough as far as memory requirements to allow you to paint quickly. If you are going to be drawing directly on the computer, make sure that your output resolution is set when you create the image. Most of the imagery you will paint will probably start at fewer than 1,500 pixels in the largest dimension.

2. Once you have set your resolution and have a basic design ready, you are ready to move on. A pencil-sketch scan usually contains a large range of gray values, as will a sketch drawn directly in the program. In this particular case, the drawing paper had numerous small, colored flecks. These types of things left in the sketch can be distracting and should be made less distinct, if not eliminated. If not much variation exists between the strokes that you are drawing with or in your scan (i.e., the sketch is predominantly black and white), you may want to skip this step. If the sketch contains lots of distracting marks and you want to remove them, use the Levels command (Image > Adjustments > Levels) to reduce the number of gray values while leaving the image looking cleaner without the speckles, as shown in Figure 15.2.

3. Save your file—I cannot emphasize this step enough. Make it a habit to save numerically named versions of your work. One of the best things about digital painting is this ability to save multiple versions to which you can revert if you make a major mistake.

FIGURE 15.1   The beginning sketch.

FIGURE 15.2   The sketch after we used the Levels command.

4. Cut and paste the image back into the original.
5. Set the Composite Blending mode to Multiply, as shown in Figure 15.3. This provides a top layer where the white has become transparent, allowing you to paint on the background layer while showing the original sketch through the top layer.

FIGURE 15.3   Converting the layer's Blending mode to Multiply.

6. As a general rule, it is not recommended that you paint on a white background. The reason for this is simple. Against a white background, especially on the computer monitor, virtually every color and value will look too dark. Therefore, you should always add a tone of color to the background of the image. In Photoshop, fill the background layer with either a color or a gray value, as shown in Figure 15.4. We chose the color in this case to contrast with later colors that will be added as we paint. You could add a gradation if you prefer.

7. Create a new layer for this next step. In Figure 15.5, a red color has been added into the turban area on the new layer. Always, when painting an image with a substantial amount of skin, begin by painting in some of the surrounding colors. These colors will influence the choices you will make as you pick colors for the skin areas. The reason for painting on a new layer will become apparent should you need to make corrections later in the painting. It is much easier to fix errors if the main elements of your painting are separate entities. Most of the painting in this image is done using only two or three brushes. The main brush used is the default brush, Airbrush Pen Opacity Flow. We tweaked the size and settings of the brush slightly as needed.

FIGURE 15.4   Adding color to the background.

FIGURE 15.5   Painting color into the turban.

8. Create another new layer, as shown in Figure 15.6, and begin adding the skin colors. You must go to the Color palette and select the individual colors that you want to use because the image contains limited colors. At this point, experiment with finding colors that you actually want to use. Begin by picking the darkest colors of the skin and blocking in the whole shape of the face. Doing so will help you establish the value range of your image. Do not concentrate on laying color down only on the figure. Work all over the image in these early stages to maintain the color theme.

FIGURE 15.6   Painting in the large dark shape of the face.

9. In Figure 15.7, the planes of the face are being carefully developed as you refine and add lighter colors to the face. You do not need to try to blend the color at this time. Let the overlapping edges of the brush strokes be the areas where you sample the colors you paint with.

10. Notice in the close-up of the painting in Figure 15.8 that some of the underlying background color shows through the skin colors that are being painted. This is particularly apparent in the temple area of the head. Try to get some of your background colors into the figure and, if possible, some of your foreground colors into the background. Do not be concerned with "staying within the lines." Notice in Figure 15.8, particularly within the circled area, the high saturation of the colors in the flesh. Notice, too, that the purple is reminiscent of the color of the turban. This is why you paint the colors surrounding the skin at the beginning.

FIGURE 15.7   Defining the planes in the face using lighter colors.

11. Begin sampling some of the colors within the image itself using the Eye-dropper tool and painting with those sampled colors. (Photoshop's hot key for the Eyedropper tool is Alt; using the hot key makes it very fast to sample and go back to painting.) You will still need to go to the Color palette for some colors, but more and more you can simply sample colors that are being created in the painting.

12. At this point, you can merge the sketch layer and the layer on which you are painting the skin color. Because the drawing layer is in Multiply mode, it will merge with the color layers and turn white. Using the Magic Wand tool, we can select most the white and simply delete it. Use the Eraser tool

FIGURE 15.8 Notice the intense color and the different colors in the face, as you can see in the circled area.

to finish the cleanup. Continue to refine the drawing while painting in more detail and gradually covering the sketch. Figure 15.9 shows a close-up of the face. Notice that you can see some of the sketch only in smaller areas, as it is covered in the painting process. This is most noticeable around the mouth.

13. Figure 15.10 shows the entire painting and how the features are being refined and developed. Notice how simply the eye is painted. There is no need at all to paint every eyelash. Also be aware of the subtle but noticeable color change in the corner of the eye. If you simply use a dark brown or black for all of your darks, you will end up with an image that looks dead. Notice the highlights that are being developed on the skin, particularly on the tip of the nose and the eye; this is where the background color is now being integrated into the overall skin color in a most dramatic fashion. This is just a matter of using the background color as the highlight. In dark-skinned people, the highlights on the skin are generally much more specular and shiny than in people with light or pale skin.

FIGURE 15.9   The merging of the sketch and painting layers.

14. Using the same brush, continue to paint the rest of the head. As you can see in Figure 15.11, you gradually and ever so slightly cool the warmer colors of the face using the blue green of the background. The shadows of the figure vary from warm to cool. Varying the colors of the shadows will keep the figure looking alive. Refine the contour of the face and the shapes of the shadows. Work your strokes across the form, meaning that the strokes are perpendicular to the long axis of the body part being painted. This is most noticeable in the neck of the character.

15. The underlying sketch is just about painted over completely by this time. Continue smoothing and refining the face, adding highlights where appropriate and blocking in some color in the background. Remember, the highlights should take on the cast of the surrounding color (or, in this case, a slight blue). Some serious consideration now needs to be given to the background area of the painting. The background is a combination of flesh tones

FIGURE 15.10   The background color being used as the highlight color.

FIGURE 15.11   Refining the painting and working your strokes across the form.

mixed with the background color, some blue/purples, and some reds to bring in some of the turban color. Begin to establish the shadow patterns in the turban, separating the light side from the dark side (Figure 15.12).

16. Figure 15.13 shows a close-up of the face so you can see all the color and general simplicity of the brush strokes used to paint.

FIGURE 15.12   Adding the background and the value patterns in the turban.

17. Additional work is now concentrated on the turban (Figure 15.14). Merge the turban layer. Using the same brush, refine the lights and darks and cover the sketch as you build up the color. Also work on the golden scarf that is hanging behind the turban on the character's head.

FIGURE 15.13   A close-up of the face.

18. In Figure 15.15, you are pretty much finished with painting the face. You should now have the background painted. The turban is painted with enough detail that the viewer will understand what it is, yet it will not compete with the face for attention. The very top of a shirt is painted.

19. The portrait needs one more thing to make it more intriguing, and that is some jewelry. Create a new layer and paint a pair of earrings on your figure. Create a second new layer and paint the large and very shiny hat pin on the turban. Use multiple layers if you need to. There is really no reason to try to paint the jewelry with great amounts of detail. Just paint them enough to give the impression of shiny metal and stones. Have a lot of fun painting the

FIGURE 15.14   Painting the turban.

FIGURE 15.15   The finished face.

jewelry, but try not to overstate them, as you want them to add interest to the face and not compete for the viewer's attention. Save your file and you are done, as you can see in Figure 15.16.

FIGURE 15.16 The finished face with earrings and hat pin.

Conclusion

That's about it for painting a face. Remember to work at low-opacity settings so that the colors can build themselves slowly and with subtle transitions. The procedures you have learned here are applicable to virtually any type of face, from alien to any human face that you can imagine. In the next chapter, we will paint long, dark hair.

PAINTING HAIR

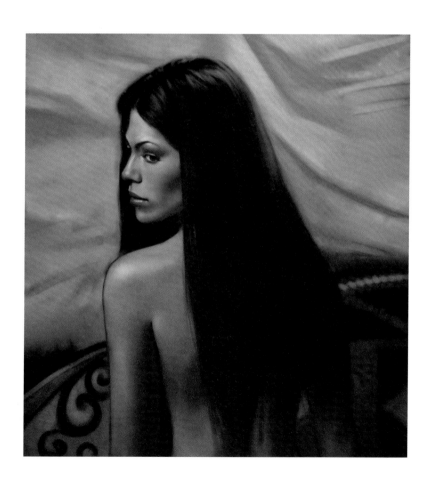

Hair is not as hard to paint as it may seem. This chapter will show you how to paint one type of hair. Because it is difficult to paint just hair without painting a face, this chapter will also review the basics of painting a face. The secret to success for painting hair is to not get caught up in all of the small details, namely the individual strands of hair. Hair is usually simple variations of the skin's colors. Stay away from using too much yellow when painting blond hair. Instead, use lots of yellowish grays with muted browns and with touches of yellow in the highlights. Red hair has lots of oranges and purples in the light areas. The highlights on black hair often appear bluish. The same is true for dark brown hair but not to the same degree. In this chapter, darker brown hair will be painted being lit from both the side and with a strong backlight.

WHAT YOU NEED TO KNOW ABOUT PHOTOSHOP FOR THIS CHAPTER

For this chapter, the special things you need to know about Photoshop CS3 are

- Where individual palettes are located
- How to create and manipulate individual layers
- How to adjust a brush's opacity
- How to resize your brush and sample color from within the image (preferably using hot keys)

TUTORIAL 16.1   A TECHNIQUE FOR PAINTING LONG, DARK HAIR

The best process is to paint both the hair and the face at the same time, but for the sake of this tutorial, we will work up the face quickly and put most of our emphasis on the hair. Figure 16.1 shows the most basic sketch done in Photoshop.

You could, of course, do the initial sketch and scan in your image to work on. This image is only meant to establish the position of the figure and the general areas that will be light and dark.

When you have your sketch in Photoshop, either by scanning or drawing in the program itself, take some time to refine the image a bit more. There is an inherent danger here. You want to refine the sketch to become more familiar with your subject, but you do not want to get a drawing that is so finished that all you do is a digital coloring book exercise. In particular, with this exercise, we want to show the

FIGURE 16.1   The basic figure sketch we will be working from.

patterns within the hair that will be painted. When painting, you must always be willing to make changes and corrections to your work. Figure 16.2 shows the sketch that has been developed a bit further.

At this point, the fun begins. The first thing to do is to get rid of all the white in the background. You will remember, as mentioned earlier, that this is the most important initial step. If you paint on a white background, all of your colors will look too dark.

1. Select the entire image and copy and paste it back into the canvas. This will leave you with a sketch on the canvas for the background and a duplicate drawing on a new layer. Change the blending mode of the layer to Multiply. This will turn all the white areas transparent while leaving the sketch visible. Make the background layer active and from the Filter menu, select Render

FIGURE 16.2   The sketch in a more refined state showing the patterns in the hair.

> Lighting Effects. In this case, two lights are applied to the background image. The top is a warm color, and the bottom is cooler. Figure 16.3 shows the sketch with the lighting effect applied.

2. Remember to save your file at this point. We cannot emphasize enough that you must always remember to save your files. Make it a habit to save numerically named versions of your work. One of the best things about digital painting is this ability to save multiple versions that you can revert to if you make a major mistake.

3. Begin to block in the darker areas of both the face and hair. Always try to establish your value patterns as early in the painting process as possible. Work on the dark colors of the face and on the dark colors in the hair using the same color and brush. In this case, use an enlarged version of the Airbrush Pen Opacity Flow brush. It is best to work on the skin and the hair

FIGURE 16.3   Applying the lighting filter to the background layer of the painting.

concurrently so that both develop in visual continuity. Figure 16.4 shows the process of filling in the darker areas of the painting. Notice that there is not a lot of concern about "staying in the lines."

We will be using the Airbrush Pen Opacity Flow brush for the majority of the work in both the hair and skin. Continue painting in the darker colors of the hair and skin, as shown in Figure 16.5. Set the size of the brush to about twice as large as you think you need it. This will prevent you from going in and drawing all of the small details. The goal at this stage of the painting is to get the larger value patterns painted in; we're not concerned about the small individual strokes. Also at this point, begin to develop some of the color in the background.

4. The steps we've done up to this point are only concerned with value. Now we will begin to concentrate on color. This involves adding color to both the skin areas and the hair. Notice that most of the colors that are in the skin are

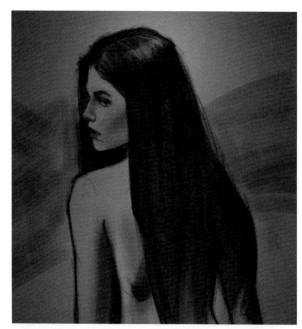

FIGURE 16.4   Beginning the initial block in of the darker areas in the painting.

FIGURE 16.5   Getting all the darker color and value into the hair and face and the start of work in the background.

also used in the hair, with only value changes apparent. Save the image. Continue to work additional colors into the background. At some point, you will be adding some of the background colors into the foreground and vice versa, as shown in Figure 16.6.

FIGURE 16.6   Adding color into the figure, hair, and background.

5. Sample color from the lighter areas of the hair and then lighten it slightly in the Color palette; paint in some light touches into the lighter side of the hair. Darken and reestablish the darker areas in both the face and the hair, as shown in Figure 16.7.
6. Using the same brush but setting it with slightly more opacity, paint in the general hair color over the whole of the head, as shown in Figure 16.8. Do not paint in individual strands of hair, and try not to cover the forms in the hair that you have developed in the earlier steps.

FIGURE 16.7 Painting some lighter and darker touches into all of the hair and skin.

FIGURE 16.8 Painting in the general, overall color of the hair.

7. Now switch back and forth between some lighter and darker colors to reestablish and clean up the edges of the hair. Sample some of the light bluish-gray color from the background and paint highlights into the hair. Also paint and tweak some of the smaller details in both the hair and face that you have not been as concerned with up to this point. Add more color and work it into the background, as shown in Figure 16.9.

FIGURE 16.9   Adding some highlights into the hair using background colors.

8. Begin to refine areas of the hair. In this case, we're working on the front strand of hair that is hanging over the shoulder. Use a slightly smaller brush, but not too small because it is still too early to be adding individual strands (Figure 16.10). As you can see, some work needs to be done in the skin areas, specifically, in the lower back area where the hair covers the skin.

9. In this painting, the head is strongly backlit. This means that there is a light source behind and, in this case, slightly above the subject. Because of this

FIGURE 16.10   Painting on the front strand of hair hanging over the shoulder.

lighting arrangement, strong highlights will appear on the hair on the top and to the back of the head. A critical thing to remember when painting hair is that it is shiny. Individual strands of hair, though shiny, will not reflect enough light to make a difference; however, when hair is massed together, all the small highlights will group together and form large, dramatically lit areas. Things that are shiny in a painting will reflect the colors of the surrounding environment. In this painting, the highlights in the hair are painted using the light colors of the background. Figure 16.11 shows the highlights strongest toward the backlight and slightly smaller as you come forward on the top of the head.

10. As the hair becomes more refined, add smaller strands. Continue to work both the hair and the skin on the shoulder and back areas where the two meet. Though this tutorial is not about painting the background, go ahead and add more color and refine shapes behind the figure to give a sense of an environment (Figure 16.12).

FIGURE 16.11   Adding dramatic highlights into the hair using background colors.

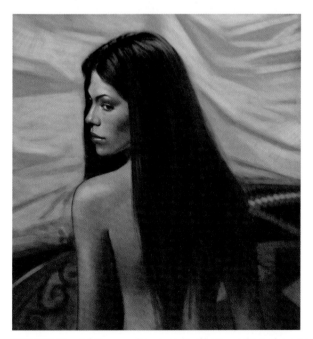

FIGURE 16.12   Adding smaller strands of hair, working the areas where the hair and skin overlap, and painting the shadows in the drapery.

11. More work is done in the area of the drapery by adding more detail and blending some of the edges. Also, include additional painting on the back, arm, and hair, as shown in Figure 16.13.

FIGURE 16.13   More work in both the drapery and skin and hair.

12. Occasionally, you may find that you want to increase the richness of the appearance of the colors that you are painting with. An easy way to accomplish this is to select your image, copy it, paste it back onto itself, and change the Blending mode to Multiply. This initially leaves a very dark image, but by adjusting the Opacity slider, you will be able to get a slightly darker but much richer-looking painting. When you have the amount of change you want, save the file in case something goes wrong and then merge the two layers. Save your work again. Figure 16.14 shows the result of this process. The image is slightly darker and richer looking.

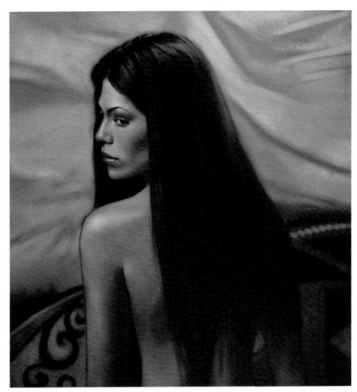

FIGURE 16.14   The result of copying, pasting, changing the blending mode, and merging the two layers of the figure.

13. Using the same brush you have been using, begin to clean up the contours of the figure and hair. Also, blend the colors both in the figure and the drapery, as shown in Figure 16.15.

14. Refine the painting in additional areas. In this case, significant work was done to paint the back where it meets the hair, as you can see in Figure 16.16.

15. Now and only now is the time to add some individual strands of hair if you want. By now, the major planes and forms of the hair are painted, and unless you go overboard, adding a few individual small details will not harm the image. Be careful, though, not to add light hair into the darker areas and vice versa. Doing so will begin to flatten the form and add visual holes to the image. The majority of the work in this image is done where the hair meets the background and in the front where the hair hangs next to the face (Figure 16.17).

FIGURE 16.15 Cleaning up the figure's contours and blending colors in both the skin and drapery.

FIGURE 16.16 Finishing the area where the hair meets the back.

FIGURE 16.17   Adding some individual and detailed strands of hair to the painting.

16. The last thing we need to do is work on the background so that it has some finish to it. Abstract or something a bit more realistic, it does not matter, as long as you handle the background with the same care as you use for the main figure. After the background is painted, paint a few wisps of hair on the sides of the head overlapping the background to achieve that finished look, as shown in Figure 16.18.

FIGURE 16.18 The background is painted using custom brushes.

Conclusion

Now wasn't that simple? The steps we just followed were meant to show a very simple way of painting one kind of hair. As you know, there are as many different types of hair as there are people. Add to the equation that many colors of hair are not natural, and a whole book could be written on just painting hair. However, if you remember the simple theory behind the process, any style of hair will be easier to paint. In the next chapter, we will again paint a face, but with a difference. Instead of painting a face with a flawless complexion, we will paint one that has many small imperfections, more like in the real world.

PAINTING FISH FACE

Y ou may be wondering why we're devoting so much time to painting with textures. Well, one of the biggest complaints you hear about digital art is that it looks too slick, that it is so perfect it has no soul or life. While the main goal of the remaining chapters of this book is to show various methods of painting different types of characters, they also aim to show that digital art need not be sterile. The goal is not to try to emulate traditional techniques but just possibly to invent a new type of image that, while obviously digital in execution, is not boring to look at.

This chapter builds on the things learned in the previous chapters. The basic information that was presented there will not be repeated here. We will also use a couple of features that we have not used before in the Liquify filter and the Quick Selection tool, so if you are not familiar with these tools, please consult the Help file or Photoshop documentation.

WHAT YOU NEED TO KNOW ABOUT PHOTOSHOP FOR THIS CHAPTER

The following tutorial assumes that you know some fundamentals of working in Photoshop CS3 or previous versions of Photoshop. You should know such things as

- Where individual palettes are located
- How to use the Quick Selection tool and where it is located (specific to Photoshop CS3)
- How to adjust a brush's opacity
- Where the Liquify filter is located
- How to create layers and change their composite method
- How to resize your brush and sample color from within the image (preferably using hot keys)

TUTORIAL 17.1   ## PAINTING FISH FACE

When you're ready to start painting this rather strange character, follow these steps:

ON THE CD

1. Open Photoshop and create a new image file or open a scanned image. The original image painted for this chapter was sketched in pencil and scanned in at 300 dpi, resulting in an image 1,000 pixels wide by 1,000 pixels high. This sketch in Figure 17.1 is on the CD-ROM if you want to use it as the basis for your painting.
2. Using the Image > Adjustments > Levels menu command (Figure 17.2), move the dark point and light point indicators until the sketch lines are nice and dark and the background is white and all gray tint is gone (Figure 17.3). We now have a sketch that is nice, contrasty, and a good basis for the rest of the painting. The sketch feels a bit crowded, so using the Canvas Size command, we add some space around the sketch (Figure 17.4).

FIGURE 17.1   The initial sketch scanned into the computer.

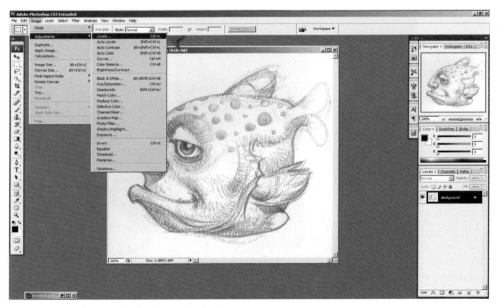

FIGURE 17.2   Adjusting the levels in the sketch.

FIGURE 17.3   The sketch after adjusting the levels to increase the darks and get rid of the gray background.

FIGURE 17.4   A bit of space is added around the sketch using the Canvas Size menu item.

3. Now we are going to have some fun using the Liquify filter. Using the Liquify filter is a great way to get multiple new and creative variations of sketches or ideas you are developing. I recommend its use whenever you are doing conceptual work or there is a need to expand an idea. Not only is Liquify a great

way of generating multiple ideas, but it is a lot of fun. The one danger is that it can be so much fun that it may become a distraction. Having given that warning, let's use Liquify to get some variations of the fish character in the sketch. In the Layer menu in Photoshop, duplicate your background sketch four or five times. We can also use the keyboard command Ctrl+J to accomplish the same thing. Never use Liquify or any filter or effect on the original layer or image, just in case there is a mistake. Always work on a copy of your image or a duplicate layer. Make sure that one of the duplicate layers is active and select Liquify from the Filter menu (Figure 17.5).

FIGURE 17.5   The Liquify filter.

The Liquify filter opens in a new window showing your image and multiple tools and options. The option you will probably find most useful is the Forward Warp Tool. This tool lets us push and pull the pixels of the image into new and interesting variations. Very often we will come up with an image that is completely different in feel and expression from the original image. We want to have accurate control over the warping of the image, so, in the Tool Options, lower the Brush Density and Brush Pressure to about 30. It is also a good idea to start warping the image using a large brush and gradually reducing the brush size as you get more into the smaller details of the image (Figure 17.6).

Push and pull the image until you have something you like. There is no right or wrong way to do this. If you need to undo some of the changes you

FIGURE 17.6   The location of the Warp tool and its Options panel.

have made while warping the image, use the Reconstruct Tool (Figure 17.7). When you have a new image that you like, click the OK button. The warping is applied to the currently active layer.

FIGURE 17.7   The Reconstruct tool.

Select the next duplicate layer and use the Liquify filter to create another variation of the original sketch. Figure 17.8 shows the original sketch in the center of the image and the variations created using the Liquify filter surrounding it.

FIGURE 17.8   The original sketch surrounded by a number of variations created quickly using the Liquify filter.

4. Decide which image you are going to use. Sometimes the choice can be a difficult one, but often there is one that just sticks out as the favorite of the bunch. In this case, I chose the variation that is right above the original in Figure 17.8. Copy and paste your selected layer into a new image. Adjust the position of the layer in the new image to give you a nice balanced look. Sometimes the individual layers in the original image are off center after warping. Figure 17.9 shows the new image. The central character has been moved to the left-hand side of the canvas to give more room to eventually paint in the tail, which has not been fully developed in the sketch. Flatten the image so the sketch is on the Background layer and save the image.

FIGURE 17.9   The new image created from one of
the Liquify variants.

5. Create two new layers over the Background layer containing the sketch.
Change their blending mode to Multiply, and on one layer paint the fish
and on the other paint the background color. Figure 17.10 shows the image
with the fish and the background painted. The painting should be quick and
is used to establish the overall color scheme.

FIGURE 17.10   The image with the fish and the background loosely
painted.

6. Create a new layer above the other layers and leave its blending mode set to normal. Use a brush of your choice to paint in more of the fish's body. For the majority of the painting in this image, I have used the Airbrush Pen Opacity Flow 19 brush. In this step, we are trying to establish more definition in the colors of the fish. Do not worry as you cover some of the original sketch. By the end of the painting all of the sketch will be covered, and you do not want to go into a "fill in the lines" mode of thinking and painting. Apply a gradient to the background to give it more life and variation (Figure 17.11).

FIGURE 17.11   A bit more painting on the fish and a gradient applied to the background.

7. Continue painting on the fish and cleaning up the contour of both the fish and background (Figure 17.12).
8. Begin developing some character in the character's face. We are still using the same brush but changing the Opacity, Flow, and Size as needed. Figure 17.13 shows the progress in the face. Always keep in mind the direction of the light source as you paint. In this character, the light is from above, and this will influence where the shadows are located.
It is worth noting at this point that there is a highlight in the eye of the fish. We are so used to seeing this highlight that it probably does not occur to the

FIGURE 17.12 More painting and cleaning up the fish character.

FIGURE 17.13 A close-up of some of the details being painted in the fish's face.

viewer that this is incorrect when you are painting a character or fish under-water, as in this case. This highlight generally indicates a wet surface in the at-mosphere, but everything underwater is in a wet environment and does not reflect this way at all. Fish underwater do not have reflections in their eyes. Because we are so used to seeing this though, we can get away with this visual inconsistency. Small visual tricks add interest and spice to an image.

9. The rest of the fish now needs our attention. Using the same brush, paint the fins and body. We are still in the early stages of painting, so do not overdo the detail but strive to get in the general shapes and colors (Figure 17.14).

FIGURE 17.14   Additional work on the fish body and fins.

10. Paint more detail into the fish to help develop the form and color further. Paint additional red into the fins and lighter creamy colors into the face and body of the character (Figure 17.15).

We are still using the Airbrush Pen Opacity Flow 19 brush at varying sizes and opacities. For most images that you paint, it is a good idea to only use a few brushes in each. If too many different brushes are used, there will be visual confusion in the painting, much the same as if a designer used many different fonts in a book or brochure.

What is the correct number of brushes to use in each painting? There is really no hard and fast rule. Generally, I will use one brush to as many as 10. Most of the time it is about five brushes.

FIGURE 17.15   More color is painted and more of the sketch is covered.

As you paint, try to get a bit of the background color into the foreground, and vice versa. This will help maintain a color harmony that is sometimes hard to achieve otherwise. You can see this most obviously where the background greens have been used in the eye of the fish. Remember not to get into the coloring-book mindset by just filling in your original lines. A painting is a fluid creation, and you will be much more successful in your efforts if you don't try to fill in your own lines. Your lines are probably wrong anyway.

11. The image now is in what can affectionately be called the "ugly stage." Almost all artists have their images go through this stage. It usually starts when you are about 17 percent into the painting and lasts almost to the end. We are mentioning this seemingly silly point for a serious reason: About this time, we might start looking at our image and tell ourselves that it will never get any better. We may be greatly tempted to simply give up and start over. Don't do that. Remember that everyone you respect as an artist goes through the same thing that you are feeling. Continue painting. If you don't, you will never finish anything and as a consequence will never improve much.

12. In Figure 17.16, we are painting some strokes on the body of the fish that follow the flow of scales, and even in this early stage there is a feeling of the fish's texture. There are also some spots added to the top of the character's back. These may or may not make it into the final image and are mainly an experiment. If they do not work, they will be painted out. Never be afraid to make a change to improve the picture. At this point, most of the original sketch is covered. There are still small bits visible around the eyes, in the nose, the mouth, the gills, and a bit in the fins.

FIGURE 17.16   Painting some strokes on the body of the fish that follow the flow of scales.

ON THE CD

13. Switch brushes to something with a little texture in it. In this case, the brush Texture1 is selected. This brush and the others used in this tutorial are available on the CD-ROM in the brush library called Book.abr. In the Brushes palette, make sure that Texture is checked. Within the Texture options, select the Pattern/Fish Scales Small as the active pattern and make sure that the Mode is set to Color Burn if it is not already (Figure 17.17). This will be the brush used to paint in all the fish's scales.

FIGURE 17.17   Settings for the brush that will be used to paint the fish scales.

14. Create a new layer. Using the Texture1 brush and sampling colors from the fish's body, paint in some scales. Figure 17.18 shows the painting of the scales on a lightened version of the body so you can see the effect easily. The scales on the top of the fish are painted using the pattern as it loads default in the Brushes/Texture options. The scales painted on the bottom of the fish have the inverted box checked. Experiment to get various looks.

FIGURE 17.18   Painting the fish scales on a lightened version of the body so you can see the effect easily.

15. Because we do not want the painted textures to be the same opacity and strength all over the character, use the Eraser tool to subtly clean up the contours and blend the scales into the rest of the painting. The results of painting the scales are seen in Figure 17.19. Do not flatten the image, but remember to save the image.

FIGURE 17.19   The results of painting the scales.

16. Duplicate the fish scales layer. Change the Blending Mode of the duplicate scales layer to Color Dodge. The scales lighten and become much more colorful. Figure 17.20 shows the original image on the right and the new image on the left with the Color Dodge layer visible.

17. Once again we will erase carefully on the new Color Dodge layer to integrate it into the overall image. We are trying to give some shine and sparkle to the scales located on the side of the fish (Figure 17.21). Our fish is getting close to being completed and is looking pretty good at this point.

18. At this point we could simply finish painting the fish while leaving the background very simple and call it done. It will make a much more interesting image, though, if we make the background more interesting. It will be easier to work on the background if it is on its own layer. Unfortunately the image was flattened earlier, and the background and fish are not separate.

FIGURE 17.20　A comparison between the original image on the right and the new image on the left with the Color Dodge layer visible.

FIGURE 17.21　Our fish is looking pretty good at this point.

This is a good argument for working on and keeping the layers separated until you are finished with the image. Fortunately it is not too hard for us to separate them now since the fish is not finished. Using the Quick Selection tool, quickly but carefully select the fish (Figure 17.22). The Quick Selection tool is a new tool in Photoshop CS3 and is well worth learning.

FIGURE 17.22   The Quick Selection tool.

19. When the fish or background is selected, we will use the Refine Edge menu to tweak our selection. This is another new feature in Photoshop CS3 that everyone should get to know well. Figure 17.23 shows the options menu and sliders that we will use to refine the mask we created using the Quick Selection tool.
20. When we have the mask adjusted to give us a good selection, cut and paste the fish onto a new layer. Finish painting the fish on his new layer. Figure 17.24 shows the finished fish.
21. All we have left to do is finish the background. Hide the fish layer. Create a new layer above the background layer and fill it with a new linear gradient based on the original background. We want to do this just to give us some-thing new and clean to work with. Create a new layer above this new gradi-ent layer. Using the Sketcher Soft brush, paint in some strokes that will be used to imitate the ripples on the surface of the water. Use both light and

FIGURE 17.23 Refine Edge menu.

FIGURE 17.24 The finished fish.

dark strokes. The background for the fish should now look something like Figure 17.25.

FIGURE 17.25   The new background for the fish.

22. It is safe to merge the new gradient layer with the painted layer. Soften the layer using Filter > Blur > Gaussian Blur. The effect should give us something that is similar to Figure 17.26.

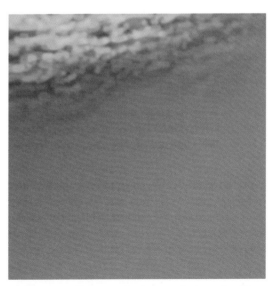

FIGURE 17.26   The water background after using Filter > Blur > Gaussian Blur.

23. Let's add some light streaks in water. Create another layer. Using the Polygonal Lasso tool, create a series of selections that will be used to represent the light beams traveling through the water. When we have completed the selection, pick the Gradient tool, select the lightest color in the water, open the color palette and make the color quite a bit lighter, and fill the sun beams on their own layer. Make sure that the gradient is set to fill with a linear gradient and that it fades to transparent instead of the background color (Figure 17.27).

FIGURE 17.27   Creating light streaks in the water to give a bit more interest and realism to the image.

24. Soften this layer using Filter > Blur > Gaussian Blur filter. Change the Blending Mode of the layer to Screen. The image will now look like Figure 17.28.
25. While we now have pretty convincing light rays streaking through the water, we can improve it just a bit more very easily. Duplicate the light beam layer and slightly offset it from the original. We have now doubled the number of light rays, and because their blending mode is set to Screen, they interact with each other and form opaque and transparent variations within themselves. Our painting now looks like Figure 17.29.

FIGURE 17.28   Softening the light rays using Filter > Blur > Gaussian Blur filter and then changing the blending mode to Screen.

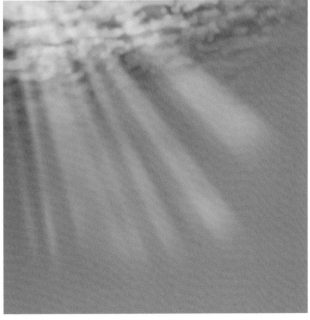

FIGURE 17.29   Duplicating the light beam layer and slightly offsetting it from the original.

26. Reveal the fish layer, and we now have for all intents and purposes a finished image (Figure 17.30).

FIGURE 17.30   The almost completed painting.

27. Often the hardest part of painting is knowing when to quit, and this piece is no exception. We are going to add one more touch that should improve the final piece. To add just a bit more of an illusion of being underwater, let's add some bubbles rising to the surface. Before we add the bubbles, select the fish layer and move it slightly lower in the picture plane to give us a bit more room for the bubbles. Create a new layer for our bubbles. Select the Bubble One brush and pick the darkest color from the water. Paint a stream of bubbles rising above the fish. Erase any that overlap our character. The image should look something like Figure 17.31.

28. We are just about finished. Create another layer, select the Airbrush Pen Opacity Flow brush, and paint a bright white highlight on each of the bubbles as in Figure 17.32. Then merge the two bubble layers and save your file.

29. For the finishing touch, we are going to make the bubbles fade a bit as they rise. To do this, make sure the bubble layer is active and create a new Layer Mask with it. Simply fill this layer mask with a linear gradient from black to white as in Figure 17.33. Notice that the bubbles now fade nicely as they rise above and behind the fish.

FIGURE 17.31   Painting a stream of bubbles rising above the fish.

FIGURE 17.32   Painting a bright white highlight on each of the bubbles.

FIGURE 17.33   Using a Layer Mask to fade the bubbles.

30. Our finished image is shown in Figure 17.34.

FIGURE 17.34   The Finished Painting.

CONCLUSION

As you can see from the final image, we have created a piece of digital art that does not scream digital when you are viewing it. At the same time, it does not mimic traditional media. It is something completely different. If you wisely and judiciously use textures in conjunction with good art skills, you will increase the beauty of your paintings. We have learned the power of the Liquify filter when we want to expand our creative reach. We have used several of the new features in Photoshop CS3, namely, the Quick Selection tool and the Refine Edges menu. In the next chapter, we will take a slight detour. Often we get stuck in a creative rut and don't know how to get out of it. Often using the same colors over and over leads to a feeling of stagnation. Sometimes something as simple as switching the colors you use will jumpstart the creative battery a bit. In the next chapter, we explore the painting process and show a virtually identical painting done in two contrasting color schemes.

PAINTING A STRANGE-LOOKING CHARACTER

This chapter covers several different concepts, including the creative use of texture—in particular, the use of texture to paint skin and background and the use of different color themes with the same subject. Many times, the skin we paint onto our characters gives the impression of an airbrushed photo. Now, someone wouldn't really mistake a painting of a monster for a photo, but much of the time the simple blemishes, scars, and flaws that make interesting viewing are eliminated or overlooked. The demonstration in this chapter will show you how to go about painting some of these types of skin effects so that you can produce a visually exciting image; it will also expand on these techniques so that you can apply them to backgrounds.

This chapter will also show the use of different color themes on the same subject matter. Why is this important? It is presented as a way to stir an artist's creativity. Often as artists we get into a comfort zone that we resist breaking out of. Sometimes this comfort zone gets boring, and we feel that we are out of ideas or our work is lacking that creative spark. Often it takes nothing more than changing something as simple as the colors we are using to break out of the artistic doldrums. This chapter will show the same subject, in this case a face, painted with two very different color schemes. While this is by no means the only way to add a spark of creativity to our work, this is often a good way to start.

Often deciding which colors to use can be problematic. If we are feeling in a rut, the colors we choose may not be different enough from the colors we normally use to give that creative spark. Fortunately, Photoshop offers an easy way to give you some new and very different colors to paint with.

The first part of the chapter will cover how to give yourself different palettes to start painting your new and more creative image. We will then take the same image and, step by step, paint it in different color schemes, finally using custom brushes to add interesting colors to both the skin and background.

This chapter builds on the things you learned in previous chapters, especially in Chapter 15, which is about painting a face. If you have not yet looked at Chapter 15, take a minute to check it out. You should also be familiar with Chapter 17, which examines painting a face using textures, because much of that fundamental information will not be presented again here.

We will be painting a rather strange-looking character so that we can exaggerate the effects and still have the look be appropriate for the subject. As expected, this demonstration is done in Photoshop CS3.

What You Need to Know About Photoshop for This Chapter

The following demonstration assumes that you know the following fundamentals of working in Photoshop CS3:

- Where individual palettes are located
- How to adjust a brush's opacity
- How to create layers and change their composite method

- How to resize your brush and sample color from within the image (preferably using hot keys)

You can arrange the Photoshop workspace to suit your own liking, so this chapter does not discuss where to locate specific items.

TUTORIAL 18.1   ## GETTING STARTED

The focus of this demonstration is twofold—creating and using a completely different palette than you are used to and, as it was in Chapter 15, painting skin. However, this time, you will learn about other techniques that will allow you to add blemishes and imperfections. While flawless skin is beautiful, it is not that common in the real world. If you can add small imperfections to flawless skin, the believability of your painting, as well as its visual appeal, will be enhanced. For some reason, things that are not pretty and perfect seem to be much more interesting to look at. We hope these techniques will make your images all the more intriguing.

First, let's create some new palettes that you can use with your images. One of the more distracting things about digital painting is the sheer number of colors you can choose from. Most artists these days have the option of choosing any of 16 million colors. That is truly an awesome amount and, quite frankly, way too many. Often, as in traditional painting, the premise of using a limited palette will serve you well in digital painting. The question then becomes, how do you limit your palette? Fortunately, this is very simple in Photoshop and depends on the Swatches palette. Figure 18.1 shows Photoshop's Swatches palette with the default 122 colors loaded. This is really quite a drop in the available colors from 16 million, yet this is really too many as well. A good number would be anywhere from 32 to 64 colors.

FIGURE 18.1   Photoshop's Swatches palette.

One of the best ways to get a completely new palette to work with right in Photoshop is to use an image in which you already admire the color scheme. Figure 18.2 shows an image that we will use to generate new swatches of color to paint with.

FIGURE 18.2   The original image used to create a new Swatches palette.

In the Image menu, select Mode > Indexed Color. This will bring up the options box shown in Figure 18.3.

In this options box, reduce the number of colors to anywhere from 32 to 64. Click the Preview box if you are curious what your image will look like with various reductions in color. It really does not matter what happens to the original image. Play with the different settings, but do not let the number of colors grow to more than 64.

We now have an image that has been reduced to no more than 64 colors, but how do you get those colors into a Swatches palette you can use? It is very simple. In the Image menu once again, select Mode < Color Table. Photoshop will display a box that shows the 64 colors that now make up the image (see Figure 18.4).

Click the Save button, and you will be presented with a box asking you for a name and a folder where you will be saving. Leave the default format as a Color Table, name the Color Table something you can remember, and save it to a location that you will also remember.

FIGURE 18.3   The Indexed Color options box.

FIGURE 18.4   The reduced palette of your image.

From the Swatches menu, select Replace Swatches and select the Color Table you just created. You will now see the colors from your indexed image loaded as your Swatches palette (see Figure 18.5).

FIGURE 18.5 The new Color Table loaded as the Swatches palette.

Now remember, we will ultimately have more than 64 colors in our final painting as we blend and push the color around. This is fine and what we expected. Starting with only up to 64 colors is our goal. To be able to create a pleasing painting with so few colors is entirely possible, as our original painting shows when reduced to 64 colors. You should create a number of different Color Tables that you will be able to load and use, but if you do not want to, a sampling has been provided on the CD-ROM in this chapter's folder.

ON THE CD

A number of small shareware programs are available on the Web that will also generate pleasing color palettes for you using different color harmonies.

Now that you have learned how to reduce an image to a minimum number of colors and have created new Swatches palettes from those colors, you are ready to start painting. The following image is painted in two ways with two different color palettes, both with 64 colors or fewer. The palettes in the top-right corner of the image are for illustration purposes only and represent the colors in the Swatches palette.

When you're ready to start, follow these steps:

1. Start Photoshop as usual. Arrange your palettes to suit your particular working methods.

2. Open the scanned sketch or create a new image that is approximately 2,000 (2,000 pixels in the largest dimension and with a resolution between 200 and 300 dpi.) Figure 18.6 shows a scanned drawing. This rather strange-looking fellow is scanned at 300 dpi.

FIGURE 18.6   A scanned image.

3. Save your result with the name of your choice, followed by "01." Make it a habit to save numerically named versions of your work. One of the best things about digital painting is this ability to save multiple versions that you can revert to if you make a major mistake.

We are first going to paint the sketch using a cool color scheme with just a few warm, complementary colors thrown in for good measure. Analogous colors are those that are located next to each other on the color wheel, while complementary colors are those located across the color wheel from each other.

TUTORIAL 18.2   **PAINTING A FACE USING A COOL COLOR SCHEME**

ON THE CD

Select Load Swatches in the Swatches palette and open a cool palette that you have created from another image or by hand. If you would rather use the swatches that were used in the creation of the tutorial image, you can load the swatches from this chapter's folder on the CD-ROM.

The first thing we need to do is get rid of all the white in the image and set the base color we want to build the image around. Select, copy, and paste the whole image back into itself, or, alternatively, you can use the keyboard shortcut Ctrl+J to duplicate the base layer. You now have two layers with identical images on each.

Select one of the blue colors from the Swatches palette. It is generally a good idea to start with a color that is located between the ends of the palette instead of one of the colors at the extreme end. This will make achieving color harmony easier as you paint. When you have selected the color, click on that color in the toolbar. This brings up the color picker. Do not move the small circle to change the color. All you are going to do here is note the RGB, HSV, or LAB values for this particular color. There is no reason to worry about the CMYK values now. Figure 18.7 shows the color picker and where you can find the RGB values for the selected color. Either remember these values or, better yet, write them down on a piece of scrap paper, as we will need them in just a moment.

FIGURE 18.7   The color picker with the RGB values highlighted.

With the background layer active, select Lighting Effects from the Filter/Render menu. In the Lighting Effects options box, click on the Light Type color box. This will take you back to the color picker. Enter the RGB values that you wrote down previously in the RGB boxes here and click OK. Set the Light type to Omni and place this light as shown in Figure 18.8.

Adjust the intensity to your liking and click OK. Your painting should now look something like Figure 18.9.

You should have two layers. The top layer's blend mode should be set to Multiply, and this layer will only be visible should you need a guide to reestablish your drawing. For now, hide the top layer.

Create a new layer on top of the background layer. This will be where we do the actual painting of the face. It is generally a good idea to separate the painting of the major pieces of a digital painting onto separate layers. This approach will make changes much easier. Selecting colors from your loaded swatches, begin to block in

FIGURE 18.8   The Lighting Effects options box.

FIGURE 18.9   The two-layer image now looking very blue.

the colors of the face using the Airbrush Pen Opacity Flow brush. This brush is a good general-purpose brush. Figure 18.10 shows the beginning stages of painting in the character.

FIGURE 18.10 Beginning to paint the skin and hair using the swatches from the color palette.

Do not worry about details at this point, but try to cover a lot of the image as quickly as possible. Work from your darkest darks to the lightest lights. This is really a somewhat mechanical way to select color, and you should feel free to try other methods. The goal is to try to stay as true to your palette as possible, and a little variation will not matter.

You will notice that on a new layer, in the upper-right corner of the image, I have dropped in a small image made from the swatches of the palette. This is so I can simply use the eyedropper tool to select the colors and not constantly move to the Swatches palette to change my working color. This is strictly a personal choice, and you will ultimately find a method that works best for you.

Continue to paint in the skin using colors selected from your swatches. Notice that we are keeping the brightest colors in the areas where the brightest color would naturally be found in a face. These areas are the cheeks, lips, nose, and ears. Figure 18.11 shows our continued efforts.

FIGURE 18.11   Continuing to paint the colors in the face.

Now, let's quickly block in the large nose ring and burning cigar (see Figure 18.12).

Using the blending technique described in Chapter 11, at a low opacity, smooth and blend some of the color that you have applied to the face. At this point in our efforts, most of the underlying sketch is covered. If you think you are losing your drawing, unhide the top layer and check things out. Make any adjustments that you feel are necessary and turn the layer off again.

Using a reddish or orange color to imitate light that might be emanating from the burning cigar, paint in a rim light on the shadow side of the character's cheek and nose, as shown in Figure 18.13.

FIGURE 18.12 Adding the nose ring and cigar.

FIGURE 18.13 Additional work on the face.

We have been concentrating most of our attention on the face of the character, and now it is time to continue to paint the costume he is wearing as well as additional work on his arms. Once again, detail is not critical at this point, but we will try to establish most of the costume in the correct values and colors while you also block in the shapes in the arms. Back on the face, using a combination of brushes and erasers, clean up the contour of the hair. You don't want to have sharp edges everywhere but a nice mix of sharp and soft (see Figure 18.14).

FIGURE 18.14   Cleaning up and blending the face.

Paint in the iris of the eye using one of your brightest colors, in this case the brightest red you have (Figure 18.15). If you see an area that you feel is getting too rough, go back and blend the colors lightly.

Since this is a rather unusual-looking character, we emphasize that fact by adding some facial decoration. Make it whatever you like: a carving, paint, or in this case, a tattoo. Remember the most important rule: create a new layer before you do anything like this. If you do not like the decoration, you can always clear the layer

FIGURE 18.15   Painting in the clothing on a separate layer, cleaning up the contour of the hair, and putting color into the eye.

and start again without ruining any other part of your painting. Paint the tattoo in a dark color. It really doesn't matter what the shape is since the whole purpose is to add some interest to the face. Change the blending mode of the tattoo layer from Normal to Darker Color and lower the layer opacity to around 70%. These settings are completely dependent on the result, and if other settings might look better, then by all means experiment until satisfactory results are obtained (see Figure 18.16).

At this point, the image is looking pretty good, but, quite frankly, somewhat boring. This is probably because the handling of the painting has been straightforward, using only one or two brushes combined with blending. The background would also be better if it were not quite so flat and possibly a bit darker. Select, copy, and paste the entire background layer back into the image. Change the blend mode of this new layer to Multiply. This is much better, as the background has now gotten quite a bit darker and our pale friend's face stands out much better. Adjust the Opacity slider if you think the image has gotten too dark to something that you find pleasing. Remember, there is no one correct look. Selectively erase in the Multiply

FIGURE 18.16   A tattoo added to the character's cheek.

layer to expose the original image in the cigar, jewelry, and anywhere you may feel needs to be lightened. Figure 18.17 shows the painting with the background layer darkened and some areas selectively erased back to the original image. I also deleted the layer with the color palette layer, as it is really not useful anymore. All color selecting that I need to do is done within the image itself.

The skin is also too flat and lifeless. To add realism to your work and help get away from that look (which screams digital airbrush), add subtle textures to the skin. A great way to start is to add a bit of noise to the image. From the Filters menu select Noise > Add Noise (Figure 18.18).

ON THE CD

Load the face texture brushes from this chapter's folder on the CD-ROM into Photoshop.

These brushes were created specifically to add subtle textures into skin in digital paintings. When the brushes are loaded, create a new layer on top of the face layer and paint in subtle textures using colors selected for various areas in the face. Of course, we do not have to worry about any of these textures ruining the painting of the face because we are on a layer that is on top of the face layer. Figure 18.19 shows the textures painted using colors from within the figure.

FIGURE 18.17 The background layer darkened significantly.

FIGURE 18.18 Adding some noise to the face.

FIGURE 18.19   Painting some textures on the face.

Don't worry about some of the paint spilling over onto the hair or darker areas of the skin. This is very easy to correct since we are painting on a new layer. If you want to experiment and get more depth, paint multiple textures using differing blend modes, one on top of the other. When you have a number of different and interesting textures painted on the skin, select the Eraser tool and go in and clean up wherever the textures spilled over any areas they should not have.

There are only one or two small steps left before we finish. First, let's have a little fun using the Liquify filter. Flatten your image and duplicate the layer three or four times. Select the top layer so it is the active layer and from the Filter menu select Liquify. Scale the brush size to your liking and lower the Brush Density and Brush Pressure to around 30 (Figure 18.20).

FIGURE 18.20   The Liquify settings.

Go in and distort the figure in some interesting fashion. Do this with all the du-plicated layers, trying to get a completely different look to your character on each layer. This is a great way to create multiple variations of characters and creatures. Do not distort the original layer and do not distort the additional layers too much or we will have to go in and repaint some of the texture and add more noise. We always want to maintain the original image. The results of Liquifying the character can be seen in (Figure 18.21).

The final image is shown in Figure 18.22

The image is finally finished, and not only do we have one image, but using the Liquify filter, we have five finished and quite different images, all with a cool color scheme that we may not have chosen in the regular course of our painting.

FIGURE 18.21   The results of Liquifying.

FIGURE 18.22 The finished image.

ON THE CD

TUTORIAL 18.3   PAINTING A FACE USING A WARM COLOR SCHEME

In this section, we are going to switch gears completely and head in a direction that is 180 degrees from the previous image. Again, we will be using swatches either culled from an existing image or handmade. The Swatches palette used is on the CD-ROM if you care to use it.

This image, though of the same subject matter, will have a completely different feel from the previous one solely because of the colors we are using. Again, this is a marvelous way to spark creativity if you have hit a slump.

Because most of the techniques used are virtually identical to the previous image, only cursory instructions will be given with each image. Where something new is used, a more in-depth explanation will be given.

So let's start. Open the sketch you started with in the previous section and make sure that the colors you will limit yourself to are loaded into the Swatches palette. Copy and paste the entire image back into itself, change the new layers' blend mode to Multiply, and hide the layer.

Using the same technique described previously, render a lighting effect using one of the colors from the swatches to get rid of all the white in the image (Figure 18.23).

FIGURE 18.23   The rendered lighting effect.

On a new layer, block in the major colors of the face and figure (Figure 18.24). Remember, this can be rough at this stage, as you are only trying to establish the color scheme.

On the same layer, continue to refine, darken, and blend the colors where needed. Keep the brightest colors where appropriate. Add some colors in the background to contrast with the face (Figure 18.25).

Add a rim light to the shadow side of the face (Figure 18.26).

FIGURE 18.24   The major colors put into the face and figure.

FIGURE 18.25   Adding colors in the face and background.

FIGURE 18.26   Adding a rim light to the shadow side of the face.

Pick a color that is complementary to the brighter colors for interest. Paint some color in the background.

On the face layer, using a combination of brushes and erasers, clean up the contour of the hair, continue to paint the arms, and paint in the iris of the eye using one of your brightest and most contrasting colors. Finish painting the character's clothing and paint some more on the background (see Figure 18.27).

We are not going to tattoo anything onto this character, but it would be nice to have some more decoration, so let's add some more jewelry. Create a new layer and paint the stud in the corner of the nose. To duplicate this for the additional three studs, you could select the stud using the lasso tool and copy and paste it. While this is a perfectly fine solution to the problem, you will end up with a lot of layers to deal with, so let's use a different approach since we are not painting a too complicated image. Select the stud with the lasso tool, but instead of using copy and paste, hold down the Ctrl and Alt keys (PC) and drag a copy of your selection above the first stud. Continue this until you have the number you would like duplicated. Notice that one was also put up by the eyebrow. The nice thing about this technique is that all of your duplicates are on the same layer. Just make sure you know where you are placing them, or you will have to go back in and individually select each one to move. Paint any remaining jewelry you may want on this layer or an additional one (Figure 18.28).

FIGURE 18.27   Finishing the character's clothing and background.

FIGURE 18.28   Paint any remaining jewelry.

This background would also be better if it were a bit darker. Let's darken the background and add some interesting visual texture. Select, copy, and paste the background layer back into the image. Change the blend mode of this new layer to Multiply and the opacity to around 30%. Merge the two layers. This is much better, as the background is now quite a bit darker (Figure 18.29).

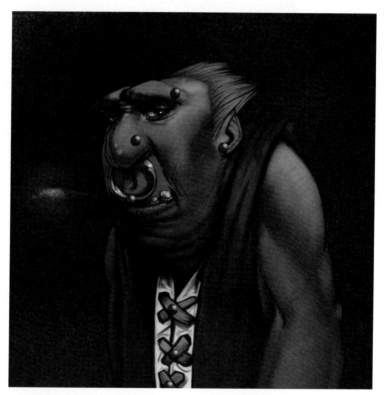

FIGURE 18.29   The background is now quite a bit darker.

The background is a bit too cool for the face, so let's warm it up. Add a new layer and fill it with a color selected from the skin of the character, change the blending mode to Color Dodge, and reduce the opacity to your taste (Figure 18.30).

ON THE CD

Create a new layer and on this layer add all the textural elements using custom brushes that you have built or the ones located on the CD-ROM. Figure 18.31 shows the image with a lighter background and textures added.

When you have finished adding the textures, merge all the background layers down.

FIGURE 18.30 Warming up the background.

FIGURE 18.31 A lighter background and textures added.

The face in this image also needs some texture added to make it more visually interesting. Using the technique described earlier, add texture to the skin. Figure 18.32 shows a close-up of the face with textures added.

FIGURE 18.32   Textures added to the skin of the figure.

Our final task is to add some depth to the textures in the background layer. Do this as described in detail earlier. To simplify, define a pattern from the entire background layer and, using layer styles, add some beveling and embossing using your newly defined pattern. Figure 18.33 shows the finished image.

In this chapter you have learned several very important things. First, we showed you a way to spark your creativity when you feel that you have lost that edge by using different and unusual color schemes that you have created from scratch or from works of art that inspire you. Second, you saw how to use texture to enliven a painting not only in the background but in something we normally would think of as smooth: skin.

FIGURE 18.33   The finished image.

CONCLUSION

In this chapter, we painted a character with a less-than-perfect complexion in two different color schemes using Photoshop's swatches. Almost always, adding some flaws and imperfections will make your paintings much more visually interesting. What you learned here is only a small portion of the possibilities we hope you will explore within your own work.

PAINTING A
FRIENDLY DRAGON

This chapter, which builds on techniques learned in previous chapters, covers two major themes: painting a rather silly dragon and using custom brushes and patterns to give a hand-drawn feeling to the painting. All of the patterns and brushes are included on the CD-ROM for your convenience. It is hoped, however, that you will learn how to create these types of patterns and brushes on your own to expand your range of creative possibilities.

As usual, the tutorial is done in Photoshop CS3. While many of the Photoshop techniques might work with other applications, their implementation may or may not be far more difficult, and some of the techniques described in this chapter, such as layer styles, really have no counterpart in other applications.

What You Need to Know About Photoshop for This Chapter

This tutorial assumes that you know some fundamentals of working in Photoshop, such as:

- Where individual palettes are located
- How to adjust a brush's opacity
- How to create and save a pattern
- How to create layers and change their blend mode
- How to resize your brush and sample color from within the image (preferably using the hot keys)
- How to create a layer style
- How to create brushes

You can arrange the Photoshop workspace to suit your own liking, so this chapter does not discuss where to locate specific items.

| TUTORIAL 19.1 | **PAINTING A RATHER SILLY LOOKING BUT FRIENDLY DRAGON** |

The focus of this tutorial is the character painted in a loose style to give a hand-drawn or scratchboard technique impression. Initially, it may seem a sloppy way to work, but the end results, if carefully done, are very attractive. Though the technique may seem complex, the digital world makes it much easier to paint than doing so would be in the traditional world. The secret of using this technique effectively is to simplify and to let the application do most of the work.

Getting Started

To begin painting your dragon, follow these steps:

1. Start Photoshop as usual. Open your scanned sketch or create a new image that is approximately 1,200 pixels in height. Figure 19.1 shows a quickly

sketched dragon with a very long and curly tail. He has been drawn directly on a new layer created over the background using the rake brush. As you can see, the sketch is far from complete, yet we're not too concerned about this because we want to further develop the idea as we paint. Do not spend hours drawing an extremely detailed sketch because you will only overpaint it. Your goal is to work smarter and not necessarily harder. The file with the sketch is located on the CD-ROM for you to use if you do not have one of your own, do not have a scanner to scan one of your sketches, or just want to follow along closely.

ON THE CD

FIGURE 19.1   The initial dragon sketch drawn on the computer.

2. If you are using a scanned sketch you have opened in Photoshop, resize the image so that it is no larger than 1,200 pixels in the largest dimension. We really do not need an image that is larger in the beginning stages of painting, as we are not concerned with small areas in the painting at this point. If needed, we will increase the size of the image as we get to the point where we are adding more detail. Always save numerically named versions of your work so you can recover your work if you make a major mistake.

3. At this point in the painting process, you need to decide what mood you want to convey in the image as well as what the main colors of the character and the environment will be. It's a good idea to do a number of color comps. These are very small images painted quickly to get a feel of the color scheme that you are looking for. They should take no longer than 5 to 10 minutes

each. Traditionally, these comps could be time consuming, but digitally there is no excuse for not doing at least one or two. In fact, once we have one comp painted, it is as easy as going to the Image > Adjustments menu and select Hue/Saturation (Figure 19.2).

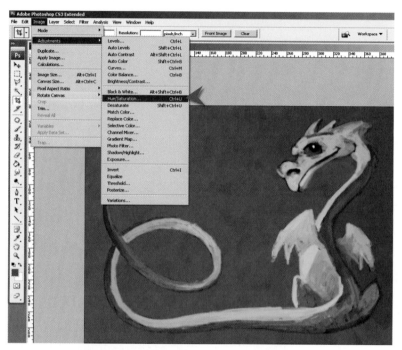

FIGURE 19.2   The location of the Hue/Saturation menu item.

Simply move the Hue slider either right or left (Figure 19.3).

We will be able to experiment with many different color schemes in a very short time. Figure 19.4 shows an example of several different color comps combined into one image.

We have decided to go with the blue comp. We will make the background a very intense blue color, and the dragon a bit more traditional green. The painting's colors will be more saturated than generally is a good idea, but since the subject matter is intended to appeal to a young viewing audience the bright colors are appropriate. The analogous color scheme will give some harmony to the painting and add interest to the composition. Do not be afraid of making a wrong decision about the colors and environment; you can change them later. At this point, sometimes the hardest part of a painting is starting. Making a few preliminary decisions will at least get you working.

FIGURE 19.3   The Hue slider used to change the colors in the color comp.

FIGURE 19.4   Four color comp variations created from one image using the Hue slider.

4. Now is a good time to decide what you are going to use as your main painting tool. This decision, though not a fundamental decision for the outcome of a successful image, most likely will affect several other steps in the painting process. For most of the painting in our blue character image, we will be using the Rake brush in various sizes and opacities; this custom brush is available on the CD-ROM. If you cannot see this brush in the Brush Preset Picker, make sure that you have loaded the Book.abr file from the CD-ROM. This brush is specifically made to paint with multiple parallel lines, somewhat imitating a scratchboard rake tool. It is a good brush to use whenever a cross-hatching pattern or technique is desired.

Removing the White Areas in the Image

After you have made your color comp and thought about what you will do, it's time to get rid of the white areas in the image. Doing this is easy, and there are a number of simple techniques to accomplish this. This section discusses commonly used ways.

The image of your character should already be on a new layer. If it is not, you need to cut and paste the sketch from the background onto a new layer. Double-click on the layer and name it Sketch or something similar. Hide the layer you have just created so it is not visible at this time. Create a new layer, drag it under the layer with your creature's sketch, and fill the layer with a bright blue color using either the Paint Bucket Tool alone, rendering a lighting effect using Filter > Render > Lighting Effects over a colored fill, or using the gradient tool. Be aware that the Lighting Effects filter will not work on a transparent layer. We have decided to use a Gradient and fill the layer with a darker blue to lighter blue color ramp. These colors will harmonize well with the main character. The layer is filled with an opaque gradient of light and dark blue colors. Make sure that the sketch layer is active. If you used the image on the CD-ROM or drew the dragon on a new transparent layer, you are set. If you are using a scanned sketch, there are a number of ways to remove the white areas of the picture:

- Select all the white on the sketch layer with the Magic Wand tool. Invert the selection. Copy and paste the selection into a new layer.
- In Channels > Load Channel as Selection (Figure 19.5), invert the selection. Copy and paste the selection into a new layer. This method gives a good copy of the sketch on a new layer, but it is usually somewhat transparent. To make the new sketch layer more opaque, simply duplicate the layer three or four times and merge these layers. We now have a nice dark copy of the sketch on a transparent layer.
- Copy the entire background layer containing the sketch into a new layer. Change the blend mode of the layer to Multiply. This not only makes the layer transparent, but somewhat increases the contrast as a whole for the image. ✄

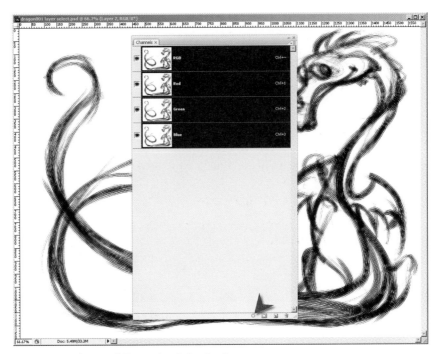

FIGURE 19.5   The Load Channel as Selection button.

TUTORIAL 19.2   **PAINTING THE GREEN CHARACTER**

Now it's time to paint our green friend. Follow these steps:

1. Make the layer with your character's sketch visible and change its blend mode to Multiply. This causes all the white of the layer or any white edges to become transparent. Any gray edges will become darker. This lets you see the original sketch over the background layer. This will become useful in later steps to check the accuracy of your drawing as you paint over the background. Create a new layer and, with one of the Airbrush Soft Round brushes, begin to block in the color for the character. This should be done on the layer that is between the background and sketch layer. Do not try to stay within the lines. It is more important to work quickly and establish the general color theme and clean up the edges later. Figure 19.6 shows the layer being painted with the Airbrush.

2. Using the Eraser tool, clean up the edges of the color that we have airbrushed on the middle layer. The sketch layer is visible to give you a guide for erasing if your airbrush strokes have expanded beyond the sketch edges.

FIGURE 19.6   Painting the green dragon on a new layer.

Figure 19.7 shows the middle layer with the edges cleaned up a bit and the top sketch layer visible as a guide. Once again, the accuracy of the edges is not critical at this point, but it is nice to keep things somewhat tidy.

FIGURE 19.7   Use the Eraser to clean up the edges of the dragon where the Airbrush brush spilled over the sketch.

3. Our little green fellow needs some more colors. Using airbrush01, paint some yellow green and some darker green areas on a new layer above the green airbrushed layer. Use the brush so it has a speckled appearance. Figure 19.8 shows these speckled areas created with the airbrush01 brush.

FIGURE 19.8   The speckled areas that are created with the airbrush01 brush.

4. Once again select the Eraser tool and clean up the edges of the character by removing some of the speckled colors painted in the last step (Figure 19.9). We can now see one of the great advantages or painting on layers. We can erase and make corrections very quickly without worrying about disturbing earlier work (Figure 19.10).

5. Now some of the real fun begins. Do not get frustrated if this stage of the painting takes a little practice. It is not hard but takes some smooth moves of the stylus along with some controlled pressure to get the look just right. Create a new layer on top of the sketch layer. This will be our top layer of the image at this point. Select the Rake brush, sample various colors from within the dragon image, and begin to develop the form and colors more. We will be covering some of the original sketch as we paint, and this is exactly what we want to do. We are trying to get rid of some of the heavy black in the drawing while still maintaining the multi-stroke feeling of the painted image. Figure 19.11 shows how the buildup of color covers the dark black lines.

FIGURE 19.9   Using the Eraser tool to remove some of the speckled colors painted in the last step.

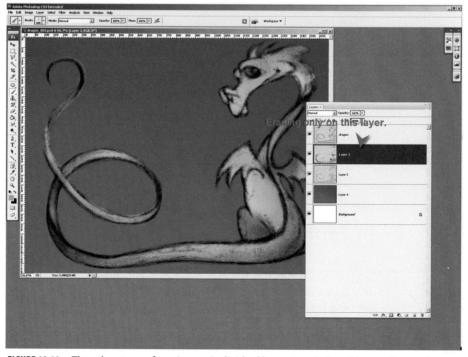

FIGURE 19.10   The advantage of erasing on individual layers is not disturbing earlier work.

FIGURE 19.11   Using the Rake brush to build up color over the dark black lines.

6. When painting both traditionally and digitally, it is a good idea to set the value range of your painting early. Begin painting with darker colors and work toward the lighter ones in your painting. Should you need to erase to clean up some of the strokes, select the Eraser tool and use the Rake brush profile with the eraser. Erase on both the color layer and the sketch layer to get a clean and controlled feeling. Do not get into the coloring-book habit of trying to stay in the lines, but do get in the habit of saving your image as you progress. The image shows some areas where the sketch layer has been erased (Figure 19.12).

7. On a new layer or on the original green layer, paint in some color for the eye. On the top layer, do as you were doing with the green and use the Rake brush paint in a bit more color. This will give the multi-stroke look and help unify the technique's appearance (Figure 19.13).

8. The dragon is feeling a little cramped in the image. There are two ways to remedy the situation. We can make the image a bit larger using the Image > Canvas Size menu command, or we can select all of our dragon layers and use the Edit > Transform > Scale command and slightly shrink the entire dragon. It is really a matter of personal preference which to use, though if we shrink the dragon too much, he may become slightly softer in appearance. In this case, the dragon was scaled down slightly without any loss of quality (see Figure 19.14). There is now a bit more space around him, making the image feel not quite as constricted.

FIGURE 19.12   Using the Rake brush as an eraser to clean up some of the black edges.

FIGURE 19.13   More painting using the Rake brush and adding some color into the eye.

FIGURE 19.14   Scaling down the dragon so he is not so crowded in the picture plane.

9. Check the image carefully if the character was scaled down. You may notice some painted pixels that were originally outside the frame and are now visible (Figure 19.15). If some of these artifacts are visible, simply erase them.

FIGURE 19.15   Artifacts left over from scaling the dragon.

10. We continue to do a significant amount of work on the character. His general color from the tip of his tail to his nose is roughly established at this point. Additional work is done refining the painted lines, changing the color of the tip of his tail and in the smaller detail areas such as the eyes and nose. Figure 19.16 shows our character at this point.

FIGURE 19.16   The color scheme of the character is established by this stage of the painting.

11. Continue to refine the color and form of the character. We have added a pointed tail, smoothed out some of the areas around the legs, added more color in the face, and generally continued to clean things up a bit. Figure 19.17 shows the dragon and reveals the level of detail and finish at this point.
12. Figure 19.18 shows a close-up of the dragon's head to show you the level of detail in the image and to show that we shouldn't overwork an image. Learning when to slow down or stop painting is just as critical with digital art as it is with traditional art. For some reason, there seems to be a greater tendency to overwork digital art.
13. Because this is a dragon, he would not be complete without being a fire-breathing dragon, so we will add some flames coming out of his nostrils. To begin, create a new layer and paint some of the yellow, orange, and red areas on the dragon that will be lit by flames coming from his nose. The yellow areas will face the flames directly. The orange flames will be painted on

FIGURE 19.17   Refining the color, brushstrokes, and shapes of the dragon. A pointed tail has been added.

FIGURE 19.18   A close-up of the dragon's head showing the level of detail in the image.

the areas that are perpendicular to the flames. The red areas will be on some of the surfaces that are not as directly lit by the flames but still fairly close to their origin (Figure 19.19).

FIGURE 19.19   Some yellow-orange reflections are painted in anticipation of adding a flame to the painting.

14. Using Erasers and Rake brushes, refine and clean up the edges of the dragon. We are at the point in the painting where we need to start taking the dragon to almost a finished state. Figure 19.20 shows the work done on the wings. Use the same amount of care on any other areas that need the attention.

15. Let's add the flaming dragon's breath. Create a new layer and, using a brush of your choice, paint in the flame coming from the dragon. When you are happy with the general shape, use an Eraser to clean up the edges and sharpen any points you may have. It is easier to use the Eraser to carve away some of the edge to achieve a sharp point than to try to paint one with a brush. Select the flames you have painted and fill them with a yellow to orange radial gradient as in Figure 19.21. Save your work.

16. Using the Rake brush in conjunction with the Eraser, paint over your flame in the same style that you painted the dragon. You can do this on a new layer if you are more comfortable working that way and then merge the two

FIGURE 19.20   Using the Eraser tool to clean up the contour even more.

FIGURE 19.21   Creating a new layer, painting a stylized flame, and applying a radial gradient to it.

layers together or just paint on the original flame layer (Figure 19.22). Once again, save your file.

FIGURE 19.22   Using the Rake brush to paint a consistent style to the flames.

17. The flame is a bit too textured, so using a softer brush, paint in some lighter and brighter yellows. Using the Soft Mechanical 48 pixels brush at a low opacity and flow setting, paint some additional bright colors on the edges of the dragon that face the flame (Figure 19.23).

18. Now it is time to begin thinking about how to handle the background surrounding the character. Right now, the background is pretty boring, and since it is only a gradient applied across the image, for the moment hide the flames we have just painted. Using the Soft Mechanical Pixel brush, paint in some magenta smoky shapes on a new layer where the flames have been displayed. This will give the impression of a hot glow in the atmosphere surrounding the flames (Figure 19.24).

FIGURE 19.23   Using a softer brush to add brighter and lighter colors to the flame and in the reflected lights on the dragon.

FIGURE 19.24   Painting a magenta glow on a new layer over the background.

19. Now create an additional layer behind the Dragon and paint in some ground using a combination of brushes while letting the Rake brush strokes be dominant. Figure 19.25 shows the ground and glowing atmosphere in the painting.

FIGURE 19.25   Using the Rake brush to paint in the ground plane.

20. Using the Rake brush, paint the entire background with strokes that are similar in style to how the dragon was painted. Try to follow some of the contours of the dragon with your background strokes. Doing this will help tie the dragon's image into the background seamlessly (Figure 19.26).
    When you are pleased with the look and feel of the painting, save your image. It may seem redundant to keep saving the image, but losing an hour's or more work can be very painful.

21. We are now almost finished creating our dragon painting. Reveal the flames and make sure that they look like you want and expect on top of the pink glow on the background. Using the airbrush07 brush with some orange color selected from the flames, stamp one or two strokes of color on a new layer on top of the flames. This adds a few sparks to the flames. If the sparks are too sharp and harsh, just soften them a bit with one of the Blur filters (Figure 19.27). Save the file and then merge all the layers together. Save the file again with a new name.

FIGURE 19.26   The Rake brush is used to paint textured strokes over the entire background, unifying the dragon and his environment.

FIGURE 19.27   Making the flame layer visible and adding some sparks to a new layer on top of the flames.

22. Now for the final step. If your merged image is on the background layer, duplicate the layer using the keyboard commands Ctrl+J or select Duplicate Layer from the Layer menu. Double-click on the new layer to bring up the Layer Style options. Check Bevel and Emboss and below that box, Texture. Select the Texture option. Pick the cross-hatch pattern, leave the scale at 100%, and set the depth to about +5% (Figure 19.28). There is now a subtle 3D effect applied to the whole image that helps accentuate all of the brush strokes you made with the Rake brush.

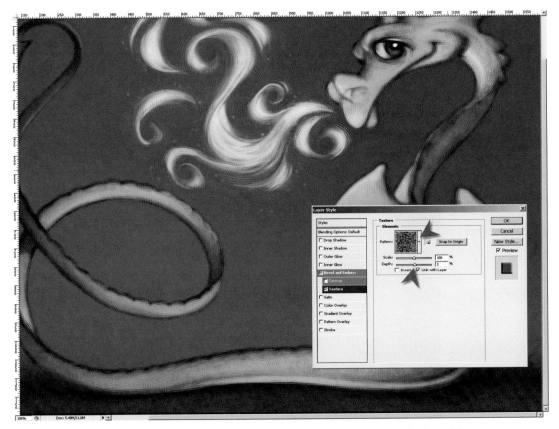

FIGURE 19.28 Adding Bevel and Emboss using Texture to a Layer Style to give the illusion of depth to the painting.

23. Figure 19.29 shows our final painting.

FIGURE 19.29   Our finished painting of the friendly dragon.

CONCLUSION

In this chapter, we used a loose technique to produce a finished painting. We used Layer Styles to create a simulated 3D look that enhanced our brushstrokes, and we used very intense colors. Not every painting you will do needs to be this intense, and generally you will want to only have a few smaller areas of intense color in any given painting. Usually too much color fatigues the eyes, but in this case it works. All in all, this is a great exercise to stretch your creative and stylistic boundaries. In the next chapter, we will be painting fabric, and, more specifically, a white gown on a female figure. We will tackle this difficult subject because you will not always be painting characters that are unclothed like we did here. Chapter 20 focuses on a very basic technique for painting one kind of cloth. Most all other types of fabric, clothing, and costume can be based on these techniques.

PAINTING THE FABRIC OF A CHARACTER'S COSTUME

U nless you intend to paint your characters nude, there is good reason to learn to paint fabric. It's possible to write an entire book about painting different types of fabric and costume, so this chapter will just describe a basic method for painting fabric.

The two most important things to remember when drawing and painting fabric are:

Draw and paint the fabric with straight lines. The thinner the fabric, the straighter and crisper the lines will be. Though fabric often forms beautiful curving lines when draped, if you draw the fabric that way, the drawing will become soft as you work the image, and the fabric will lose much of its form.

Draw and paint only the major folds that help describe the form underneath. There is a distinct difference between folds and wrinkles. Folds originate from points of tension on the figure and help generally describe the form underneath. Wrinkles are just creases in the fabric.

Another thing to keep in mind is that the material a fold is made of determines the fold's visual weight. For instance, gauze will fall into folds that are very different from leather.

Several different types of folds each have a distinctive look, including these:

- Folds caused by the action of gravity, which causes the fabric to fall on itself
- Folds that originate from objects that are under the fabric
- Folds caused by the wind

This chapter won't be covering kinds of folds. If you want to learn more about them, consult one of the good books out there that describe how folds work.

WHAT YOU NEED TO KNOW ABOUT PHOTOSHOP FOR THIS CHAPTER

This tutorial assumes that you know some fundamentals of working in Photoshop CS3. You should know such things as:

- Where individual palettes are located
- How to create and work with layers
- How to adjust a brush's opacity
- How to resize your brush and sample color from within the image (preferably using hot keys)

This chapter builds on the things learned in the previous chapters, so we will not repeat the basic information presented there.

| **TUTORIAL 20.1** | **PAINTING FABRIC** |

Let's start painting some fabric. Follow these steps:

1. Open Photoshop and create a new image file. If you do not have an image that you want to work with, the sketch that this tutorial uses is located on the CD-ROM and can be used. The original image for this painting was created approximately 1,500 pixels wide (2,000 pixels high), and a photograph was used as a reference. You could scan the image, bring it into your program, and paint over the scanned photo, but you will learn more about the process if you paint over a drawing instead. Do whatever works best for you.

2. The whole image is done with only a few different brushes, with the opacity set at various densities, and the size increased and decreased as needed.

3. We will take extra time to establish the face of the character before we draw the costume. This is not the best way to work and is not recommended. However, since this demonstration is about painting the costume, it is appropriate to get the major work on the face done first. Either draw an image similar to the sketch or open the sketch supplied. Figure 20.1 shows the sketch from a reference photo. Notice that at this point not a lot of detail is drawn into the sketch. This is on purpose to help us resist the impulse to just fill in the lines in a coloring-book style.

FIGURE 20.1   The sketch from a reference photo.

4. Apply a lighting effect from the Filter menu to get rid of all of the very bright white in the image. A greenish effect is applied to the top of the image, and a slightly violet effect is placed on the lower half of the image. We chose this lighting scheme for Figure 20.2 because we'd already decided to paint the hair a reddish color and keep the fabric slightly warmer compared to the background.

A green and violet color scheme is very easy to handle as far as how the colors interact. The lighting is applied to get rid of the white surface of the canvas and to add subtle color that will be used in the actual fabric painting. You can see some of the basic work in the face and hands. Save your file.

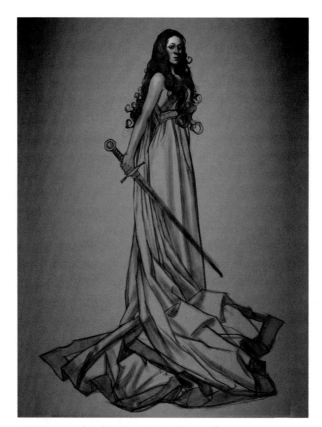

FIGURE 20.2   The sketch with a lighting effect applied.

5. Because this tutorial is about painting fabric, not much time will be spent on describing the process of painting the face, hands, arms, and sword. There is, however, value in showing the procedure as a review on how to handle these subjects. Figure 20.3 shows the face, hair, and arm of the character

being blocked in on a new layer. Notice that the sketch is not completely covered and we are not trying to "stay within the lines" of the sketch. Painting on a newly created layer makes changes and corrections very easy.

FIGURE 20.3   The face, hair, and arm of the character being blocked in on a new layer.

6. Continuing on the same layer, the hair is finished a bit more, and the hand, arm, and sword are blocked in. At this stage of the painting (see Figure 20.4), enough finish needs to be done to give a good idea of what the final image will look like, but it would be unwise to try to finish the face, arms, and hands at this early stage. Invariably, as we finished the rest of the painting, we would find we needed to go back and repaint sections, if not the entire face. Leaving the face at a more unfinished stage will make it easier to make changes as the painting is completed.

7. Figure 20.5 shows the painting to this point with the face, hands, and part of the sword blocked in. The painting is now ready for us to begin painting the fabric costume. In this case, we will actually be painting two separate parts of the costume, the dress and the cape.

8. Create a new layer for the fabric and arrange it so that it is located underneath the layer with the face on it. Change the blending mode of this layer to Multiply. Using the polygonal Lasso tool, select the area for the darker purple cape.

FIGURE 20.4   More painting, but do not overwork the figure at this early stage.

FIGURE 20.5   The image ready to have the fabric painted.

Fill this with a light bluish purple color. Select the dress proper and fill it with a light greenish gray. Last, select or paint over the golden trim on both the purple cape and white dress with a light golden color. All that we are doing at this point is setting the large color areas of the costume (Figure 20.6).

FIGURE 20.6   The large color areas of the costume are defined.

9. Create a new layer on top of the dress color layer but below the face layer and begin painting in the lights and shadows of the dress using the Airbrush Pen Opacity Flow brush (Figure 20.7).

10. On the same layer, begin painting in the lights and shadows of the purple robe using the Airbrush Pen Opacity Flow brush (Figure 20.8).

11. When the darks are blocked in, we go back into them with a slightly lighter brush and reinforce the directional folds. It is critical that when we are doing this, the color that we are using is dark enough to not punch visual holes into the darks. Try squinting your eyes at the image and see how the lighter colors merge into one shape. Figure 20.9 shows the painting as we draw in the folds of the robe.

FIGURE 20.7 Painting the lights and shadows of the dress.

FIGURE 20.8 Painting the lights and shadows of the purple robe.

FIGURE 20.9   Working some of the lighter purples into the folds of the robe.

12. We need to paint the trim folds in the correct colors, too. In this case, we will use a golden color to contrast with the purple of the robe proper. To maintain interesting contrasts, be sure to keep these golden tones lighter than the robe. Also, notice that we are not using a pure golden color but a gold that has distinctly reddish and orange casts. Figure 20.10 shows the these different color casts as we paint the trim on the costume.

13. An important thing we need to remember when painting white fabric is this: Rarely is white fabric white. This may sound like an oxymoron, but it is the truth. When you are painting white costumes, it is important to vary the colors within the fabric slightly instead of using gray values. If you paint white fabric in shades of neutral gray, your painting will lack life, and most likely your carefully painted white costume will look gray. This particular dress will pick up some of the color of both the background and the purple cape. You will notice in the shadow areas of the white gown in Figure 20.11 some rather intense and definitely not gray colors painted in to add variety and life to the white costume.

FIGURE 20.10 Different color casts in the trim on the costume.

FIGURE 20.11 Intense colors add variety and life to the shadows of the white costume.

Much of the color that is used to paint is sampled from within the image at this stage. It is also good to put these more intense colors on the transition edges from the darks to the lights. If you paint too bright a color into either the light or dark areas, you will change the perceived color of the fabric or make it look like it has dirt or stains on it.

14. As you paint, remember that the lightest lights in the fabric are closest to the center of interest, which is the face. As the fabric gets farther and farther away from the head, the values get darker. Because the major patterns that were first sketched were somewhat lost in the initial lay-in, they are reestablished and cleaned up here. Usually when painting fabric, all you will need to do is a convincing job of three values: a dark value for the shadows, a mid-value for the majority of the fabric, and a light value for the highlights. In this painting, the mid-value is more part of the dark shadow than a true mid-tone. Remember that everything is relative and that the mid-value for a white costume is not the same as the mid-value for a darker fabric. As shown in Figure 20.12, the whites closer to the face are brighter.

FIGURE 20.12   The whites closer to the face are brighter.

The folds are refined even further; use straight lines and draw with the darkest of the three values. Notice that many of the darker colors in the cape are repeated in the darks of the costume. This technique will help unify your paintings.

15. At this point, the image needs a bit more contrast. There are two ways to do this, and the easiest would be to use the Brightness/Contrast controls in the Image > Adjustments menu. I prefer to use a second method, which is to duplicate the image layer, change the Blending Mode to Multiply, and then lower the opacity to something visually appropriate. This method also increases the color saturation while giving me the freedom to erase on the multiply layer to reveal the underlying image that may not have needed adjustment. Figure 20.13 shows the image with the contrast increased a little.

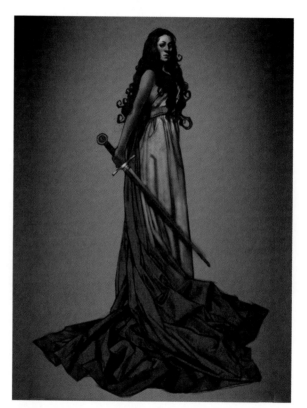

FIGURE 20.13   Increasing the color saturation and contrast using Multiply on a duplicate layer.

16. We need to add work on the background. Create a new layer under the figure and, using colors from the figure itself, paint in some background. At this point, all we are working for are value passages. You will notice that the background is slightly lighter on the shadow side of the figure than on the light side. This increases the visual difference between the lights and darks in the image (Figure 20.14).

FIGURE 20.14   The background is slightly lighter on the shadow side of the figure than on the lighter side.

17. Continue to define and refine the folds of the costume into the shadow area of the figure, as shown in Figure 20.14. Figure 20.15 shows a closer look at the continuation of some additional work in the character's face and hair. Notice the variety of colors used in the shadows. Figure 20.16 shows the whole painting to this stage.

18. Now it is time to do some additional work on the background. Using some of the large texture brushes, stamp some color on a new layer behind the figure layer and above the background (Figure 20.17). We don't need to worry about any seams or hard edges that are left since we will paint them out at a later stage. The goal here is to simply start to add some interesting textures into the background.

19. We want to continue to add interest into the plain background. Because we have painted both the face and the costume on separate layers, adding interest to the background is an easy chore. Individual layers will eliminate the necessity of carefully painting around the contour of the figure if all the work had been done on one layer. Figure 20.18 shows additional textures painted using selected brushes. These brushes and texture files can be found on the CD-ROM.

ON THE CD

FIGURE 20.15 More work on the face and hair.

FIGURE 20.16 The whole painting to this point.

FIGURE 20.17   Adding some textures to the background.

FIGURE 20.18   Even more textures are added to the background.

20. Figure 20.19 shows the entire painting with the textures in the background.
21. While a definite improvement over the plain gray background, there is still room for improvement. The texture as it stands is pretty dark and boring for the figure. There are two solutions to this problem: either we can make the figure darker or add some lighter areas in the background. As it is easier, let's add some lighter passages to the background. This is very simple to do, and we use the same brushes as we did earlier but paint in lighter color on a new layer. There is no right or wrong; just go with your own personal feeling. Figure 20.20 shows the lighter textures painted in.

FIGURE 20.19 The painting with background textures.

FIGURE 20.20 Some lighter textures added to the background.

22. The painting is now very harmonious in its color scheme. At this point, we move back to painting on the costume and figure. For some reason, it is often easier to draw a stroke in one direction than in another. For this reason, it is often advisable to rotate the canvas to make painting easier. To rotate the image, go to Image > Rotate Canvas and pick your amount of rotation (Figure 20.21).

FIGURE 20.21   How to rotate the image.

Figure 20.22 shows rotating the canvas 90 degrees clockwise to make painting the long strokes on the robe easier.

23. Switch back to the purple robe and gold trim and finish painting the fabric.
    Simplify and use three or four values at the most. Paint some of the back-
    ground color up to the fabric to help define the contours. Notice the purple
    touches in the gold shadows to help unify the complementary color scheme
    (Figure 20.23).

24. Create a new layer and paint the blade of the sword as in Figure 20.24. Use
    the Line tool to help keep straight edges. Use selections to help paint reflec-
    tions on the blade without overpainting the blade edges. We want to make
    sure that we reflect some of the purple robe colors into the metal sword
    blade.

25. Select the entire background and define it as a pattern. Double-click on the
    background layer to bring up the Layer Styles options palette. Click on the
    Bevel and Emboss button and then select the Texture button. Load the pat-
    tern you just created from the background of your image. Check the Invert

FIGURE 20.22   A rotated image is easier to paint on sometimes.

FIGURE 20.23   Finishing the fabric.

FIGURE 20.24   Painting the sword blade.

button and set the depth to an amount you find attractive. As the image updates, notice that there is a nice 3D effect applied to the textured background (Figure 20.25).

26. A few more small things and our image will be finished. Create a new layer and finish the handle and blade of the sword (Figure 20.26).

    Then paint some design on the golden fabric on the top of the gown. Using the Dodge tool, very carefully lighten the center areas of the gold to highlight and add some shine (Figure 20.27).

    Because this section is about painting fabric there will not be any additional work on the figure at this point.

27. We will crop down the image slightly because there is a lot of empty space around the character and make a final and subtle adjustment to the brightness and contrast of the painting. When finished, save your image. Figure 20.28 shows the final painting.

FIGURE 20.25   Using a pattern defined from the background to add a bit of 3D illusion to the image.

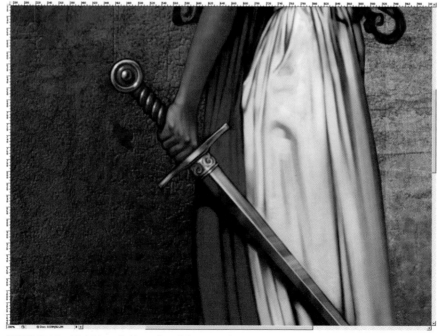

FIGURE 20.26   Finishing the handle of the sword.

FIGURE 20.27   Adding some detail to the golden fabric on the top of the gown.

FIGURE 20.28   The final painting after some cropping and subtle adjustment to the brightness and contrast.

CONCLUSION

That's about all there is to painting fabric in a very simple way. The most important things to remember when painting this type of subject matter are:

- Simplify and use only three values to do the majority of the painting.
- Draw and paint the fabric with straight lines because as you do additional work, the lines will soften.
- Paint the major folds first, do the smaller folds second, and (if you cannot stand it any longer) add some of the small wrinkles. Remember that the major folds will make the image understandable.
- Vary your values slightly as you paint across the figure.

Almost all costumes may be painted as a variation of this basic technique. Shiny objects will have greater value differences among the three values used. Furry objects will have very soft lines and transitions between shapes. If you analyze your subject carefully and use these simple steps, no costume will be too difficult to paint. In the next chapter, we will be using Photoshop's painting capabilities to paint a dragon after a heavy lunch.

PAINTING THE DRAGON'S LAIR

In this chapter, we will be painting a picture that uses most of the concepts and techniques shown in previous chapters. We will be painting an image of a dragon sitting in his cave after a rather heavy lunch. The main goal is to create a well-executed painting that is strong in composition as well as color. In combination with the artistic goals of this project is the desire to also make an image that is slightly creepy and yet humorous. This is a lot to tackle since you not only have to be a good artist but also have to know how to add expression and feeling to an image.

What You Need to Know About Photoshop for This Chapter

The following tutorial assumes that you know some fundamentals of working in Photoshop CS3, such as:

- Where individual palettes are located
- How to adjust a brush's opacity
- How to create layers and change their blend mode
- How to resize your brush and sample color from within the image (preferably using the hot keys)
- How to create and use patterns
- How to create brushes

You can arrange the Photoshop workspace to suit your own liking, so this chapter does not discuss where to locate specific items.

Tutorial 21.1   Painting the Image

The original sketch we will be working from is shown in Figure 21.1.

When you're ready to start painting the dragon's lair, follow these steps:

ON THE CD

1. Scan the original sketch at 300 dpi so that a good image can be printed directly from the image if you want. The scan was large, almost 3,000 pixels in the largest dimension. For the majority of your digital painting, this will be just too cumbersome to start with, so let's resize it to 1,500 pixels in the largest dimension. This size is much easier to handle in the initial painting stages. This sketch is located on the CD-ROM if you want to follow along using it, or you can use a sketch of your own.

   Remember that every image displayed in these demonstrations represents a saved version of the image. You cannot save enough, so don't hesitate to save constantly. You will be happy in the end that you have gotten into this habit.

2. Open the image in Photoshop and copy and paste the entire image back into itself. Hide the pasted layer; it will only be used if you need to reestablish

FIGURE 21.1   The basic drawing.

your original drawing. As shown in Figure 21.2, use the Levels command found in the Image > Adjustments menu to increase the contrast and get rid of some of the gray tones in the image.

FIGURE 21.2   The original sketch after using the Levels command.

3. Create a new layer above the background layer and fill it with a mid-value brown color. Change the Blending mode of the brown layer to Multiply. We now have an image that has a brown background that will eventually become the cave that our dragon sits in (Figure 21.3).

FIGURE 21.3   Adding a new brown layer with a Blending mode set to Multiply.

In this image, we want to create something that is humorous but just a touch dark and creepy, and our goal is to let the viewer's eye fill in many of the details. We need to make the whole thing even darker before we begin painting in earnest, so duplicate the brown layer and merge the two brown layers together. Everything is quite a bit darker now. Create a new layer above the brown layer and begin painting in broadly with a darker brown color using the Wet Sponge brush in larger sizes, as shown in Figure 21.4. Experiment with the brush using different settings to get a look that you like. Save the image.

4. Create a new layer to start painting some of the dragon's colors. Leave this layer in Normal mode. Begin blocking in some light green colors for the underside of the dragon and some darker greens for the backside and top of the creature. Use the Airbrush Pen Opacity Flow brush at fairly high levels of Opacity and Flow. The goal is to get some colors established quickly and help define the direction of the painting. Because the top layer with the sketch is in Multiply mode, the drawing is clearly visible as you paint (Figure 21.5). Continue painting all over the beast. Notice in Figure 21.5 that we are not

FIGURE 21.4   Painting darker browns into the background.

worried about staying in the lines of the original drawing. This is not important at this stage of the painting. The most important thing is to develop the
areas that will be light and those that will be dark. Save the image again.

FIGURE 21.5   Beginning to paint the green colors into the dragon.

5. Hide the top sketch layer and continue to paint on the dragon. We hide the top layer to make sure that we are painting and not just trying to fill in the shapes created by the sketch. We do not want to approach painting as if we were painting in a coloring book. Add more dark color on the brown cave layer. Using the same Airbrush Pen Opacity Flow brush start to paint some of the details in the dragon such as the teeth and spines on his back. Add a bit of orange to the eye. This will give him a slightly sinister look. As you can see, we are covering most of the original sketch that showed through the image. Never fear, since you still have the very top layer with the original sketch if you need to refer to it. Part of the fun, though, is taking the original image and pushing it beyond the sketch to create something completely new (Figure 21.6). Save the image.

FIGURE 21.6   More work on the dragon and background, including a touch of color into the eye.

6. Duplicate the dragon layer. Change the Blending mode of the duplicate layer to Multiply. Set the Opacity of the duplicate layer to about 30%. Merge the two dragon layers. We do this to get a bit more contrast, more saturated color, and a slightly darker dragon layer. The results are shown in Figure 21.7. The image is finally getting dark and moody enough. Save the image.

FIGURE 21.7   Making the dragon darker by duplicating the layer, changing it to Multiply, and merging the layers together.

7. Make sure that the brown background layer is active and create a new layer right above it. Select the Cave Rock brush and a dark brown color and stamp the image on the new layer. It is often also advisable to paint with these brushes as if they are stamps. To do this, simply touch the stylus to the image and lift it off. Do not touch and drag the stylus around. Change the layer Blending mode to Multiply. While the brush stamps a photographic image, we are not going to leave it that way and are using this as a guide to develop a painted version of the cave the dragon inhabits. The results of stamping the image can be seen in Figure 21.8. Some of the background is missing on the very right of the painting, and we will paint this in as we go. It should be mentioned that some of the major cracks in the Cave Rock brush were placed specifically to point and lead to the dragon head. This is just a subtle trick to help lead the viewer's eye where we want him or her to look. Save your image again.

8. Merge the two background cave layers. Pick Dons Sampled Brush 13 and paint the rocks on the right side of the image. Begin to paint over the photographic background. We do not need nearly as much detail as is present in the rocky wall, and we might as well start to get rid of some of it. You can see the strokes right above the nose of the character. We will be sampling colors from within the image using the Eyedropper tool to paint the different colors in these rocks (Figure 21.9). Save the image.

FIGURE 21.8   Stamping some background onto the cave layer using a large brush created from a photograph.

FIGURE 21.9   The painting with a brush that has texture over the cave background.

9. Hide the dragon layer. Using the same brush, continue to work on the cave wall as shown in Figure 21.10. We are trying very hard to keep our values in their proper place while getting a hand-painted look. We do not want to visually break apart the flow of the image by having some areas look photographic and some look painted. Save your image again.

FIGURE 21.10   Hiding the dragon layer and continuing to paint the background wall.

ON THE CD

10. Reveal the dragon and start painting back into his body again (Figure 21.11). A good brush to use is Dons Sampled Brush 2 Randomized. This brush is available on the CD-ROM.
    This brush should be set to about 50% Opacity and Flow. Sample colors from within the dragon himself and let some texture begin to show (Figure 21.12).
11. Continue to paint in the dragon. Paint in the teeth and start to clean up some of the contours of the creature. When needed, use the Eraser tool in conjunction with brushes. Much of the work at this point is being done with the Airbrush Opacity Pen Flow brush (Figure 21.13). Save the image.
12. Figure 21.14 is an example of changing direction. I am not happy with the nose and teeth of the character, so I create a new layer and begin to experiment and make changes. I paint over the nose and try adding more detail to the teeth area. It is not always a bad thing to experiment. Sometimes you

FIGURE 21.11 More painting on the dragon.

FIGURE 21.12 A close-up of the dragon showing some of the texture left by the brush.

FIGURE 21.13   Painting the dragon's teeth and more work in the chin area.

will find solutions to problems that improve an image, and sometimes you will be heading down a dead end. The main thing is that you have the courage to try and that you remember to work on either a duplicate layer or image.

13. More experimentation. This time we duplicate the dragon layer several times and Warp each duplicate using the Liquify tool. We are simply trying out some variations on our dragon to see if there is anything we like better. Figure 21.15 shows four variations of the dragon created using Liquify.

14. Having settled on the dragon variant we are going to continue using, it is time to continue developing the character and background. Things are looking pretty monochromatic in both the dragon and cave. To add interest, we will add some color variations to them. We will use Layer Masks to accomplish this task. Duplicate both the dragon and cave layers. Select one of the dragon layers and using the Image > Adjustments > Hue/Saturation command, change the hue of this dragon layer to a more blue-green than the original yellow green (Figure 21.16).

FIGURE 21.14 Experimenting with different teeth and nose on the dragon using a new layer.

FIGURE 21.15 More experimenting using the Liquify filter to change the general shape of the dragon.

FIGURE 21.16   Using the Hue/Saturation command to change the color of a duplicate layer of the dragon and background.

Save the image. Select one of the cave layers and using the same command, change the active cave layer to be more of a cool gray instead of a brown. On the top cave and dragon layers create layer masks. Fill each layer mask with a linear gradient from white to black. Figure 21.17 shows all of the layers and the layer masks.

15. Merge the cave layers together and merge the dragon layers together. The Painting will now look like Figure 21.18 with some nice color variations traveling across the images. Save the image.

16. Create a new layer over the dragon layer and paint the details of his face. His eye is painted, his nose is repainted, and some warts on his chin are added. This work is done with the Airbrush Pen Opacity Flow brush (Figure 21.19).

17. A major change is made to the legs of the dragon. Since changing the legs is an experiment, the painting is done on a new layer. Additional detail and color is added to the eye; he is given a very small pupil in a red iris to make him look decidedly more sinister. Warm touches are added to the nostrils in anticipation of adding some flames. The teeth are changed a bit so as not to

FIGURE 21.17 All of the layers and the layer masks.

FIGURE 21.18 Some nice color variations across the image.

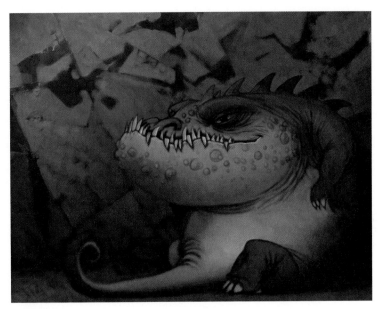

FIGURE 21.19   Painting more details of the face.

be as round or have quite as much contrast. Figure 21.20 shows all the changes made at this point. Your painting should look similar but not necessarily identical since your vision of a dragon is different from mine.

FIGURE 21.20   A major change is made to the legs of the dragon.

18. We are going to stick with the new legs, so lots of detail is painted on them including skin folds and bumps and scales. Skin folds are added in the appropriate areas all over the dragon's body, scales and bumps are added to the dragon's closest leg, the bottom of the far foot is painted, and more spines are added to the character's back. The mouth is refined, and some of the teeth are removed to give the mouth some balance. In Figure 21.21 you can see the changes made using the Airbrush Opacity Pen Flow brush with Opacity and Flow set to around 70%. All of the work is done on a new layer, which will ultimately be merged with the dragon layer.

FIGURE 21.21   More changes to the dragon.

19. We are now going to paint some scales on the dragon. This could be a very tedious job if you were doing this in a traditional medium, but fortunately it is very easy in the digital world. Create a new layer to work on. Select the Dragon Skin brush. This brush already has a scale texture associated with it, but we could change to a different texture at any time. Selecting a dark green color from the dragon's body, begin to paint scales into the slightly lighter parts of the creature. As you start to paint into even lighter areas, select slightly lighter colors to paint with. We do not want to get any jarring contrast areas, as we want the scales to appear natural. Also, remember to scale the texture down to paint smaller scales where appropriate, such as on the stomach and under the chin of the dragon. Keep the large scales on the

back and top areas of the dragon. We will use the Eraser tool in conjunction with the brush to soften some of the scales if they get too harsh. You can see the results in Figure 21.22, where the larger and darker scales are on the dragon's back and the smaller and lighter ones are under his chin. Also, notice the texture control in the Brushes palette. This is where we will change and scale the textures we are using to do the painting. When you are happy with the work that has been done, remember to save the image.

FIGURE 21.22   The Brush palette showing where you set the texture of a brush.

20. We have painted all the scales using an easy method of letting the brush do all the work, and the results are quite satisfactory. We now need to add some additional scales to refine and finish the look. The additional scales and finishing touches that will be painted on the dragon hide need to be done by hand. Create a new layer to paint on. Once again, we will be using the Airbrush Opacity Pen Flow brush to do the actual painting. Drawing inspiration from an alligator's hide, paint some large and random scales and bumps on the dragon's back. When you are happy with the result, merge all the dragon layers (Figure 21.23).

FIGURE 21.23   Some hand-drawn scales are added to the dragon.

21. The dragon is about finished at this point, so it is time to switch back and paint on the cave wall and surrounding environment. Create a new layer to paint the bones left over from lunch. Reveal the sketch layer to help refresh your memory of the placement of the bones. On the new bone layer, quickly block in their shape. On the cave layer, we continue to paint the cave wall to give it a more hand-painted look while using the original stamped brush stroke as a guide. You can see most of the work at this point on the cave wall right under the dragon's chin. While painting the dragon, we have flattened his form out. This is a typical result when painting lots of small details such as scales on the hide. We need to give him back a sense of roundness and dimension. To do this quickly and easily, we duplicate the dragon layer, change its Blending mode to Multiply, Lower the opacity of the layer to an acceptable amount, and erase everything except the areas we want to stay darker like under the chin, on the belly right under the chin, and on the bottom of the legs and back. Figure 21.24 shows the work on the cave wall, the bones blocked in on the cave floor, and some shadow added back into the dragon.

22. Using the Big Textured Chalk 1 brush, finish painting the cave wall as shown in Figure 21.25. Notice how many of the angles and lines in the rocks lead the eye right to the dragon's head. Notice also the use of the bluish colors from the left side of the image in the shadows of the rocks on the right side of the wall.

FIGURE 21.24   Painting on the cave wall, the bones blocked in on the cave floor, and some shadow added back into the dragon.

FIGURE 21.25   Angles and lines in the cave wall lead the eye.

23. Continue with the same brush and finish painting the bones as shown in Figure 21.26.

FIGURE 21.26 The finishing touches are placed on the bones.

24. We are almost finished with the painting at this point. A couple of small touches are needed to complete it. Let's paint a flame coming out of the dragon's nostrils. In this case, we will limit the flame to the back nostril. Doing this helps give the impression that our rather chubby dragon has only enough energy to flame from the one side after a rather filling lunch and adds some subtle humor to the overall painting. Use the Airbrush Pen Opacity Flow brush and possibly an airbrush, create a new layer, and paint the flame. Remember to paint some light from the flame on the edges of the dragon's face (Figure 21.27). Save the image.

25. At this point, we can go ahead and flatten the entire image. We want to add a bit of blur to the background as we get farther away from the dragon. To do this, we will use Smart Filters. This feature is new to Photoshop CS3 and is a wonderful feature that lets us apply filters to an image in a nondestructive way. More information on Smart Filters can be found in the Help file or manual. To apply the blur using Smart Filters, the first thing we need to do is convert the image for a Smart Filter. Create a duplicate layer to work with just in case, and from the Filters menu select Convert for Smart Filters. Apply a Gaussian Blur with a radius of about 2.5. Figure 21.28 shows the Layers palette with the duplicate dragon layer converted to a Smart Object and the Blur filter applied as a Smart Filter.

FIGURE 21.27   Painting the flame from the back nostril of the dragon.

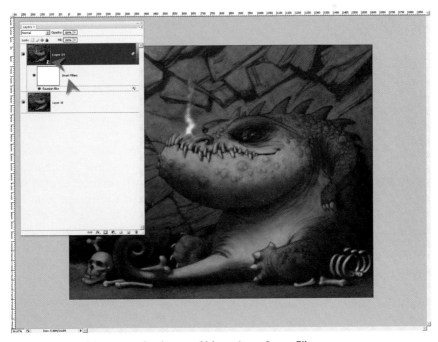

FIGURE 21.28   Adding some background blur using a Smart Filter.

26. The Smart Filter lets us manipulate where the effect is applied. Using the Eraser tool, we can paint in the filter mask to have the Blur applied just where we want it. Figure 21.29 shows the Smart Filter mask active and where it has been painted to limit the blur on the edges of the image.

FIGURE 21.29   Erasing on the Smart Filter to limit its effect.

27. Figure 21.30 shows the image after applying the Smart Filter.
28. We will apply just a hint of noise to the entire image. The noise will help minimize any subtle mistakes and make the image look less digital. From the Filter menu select Noise < Add Noise and set the amount to 2.5% (Figure 21.31).
29. Figure 21.32 shows the finished painting.
30. After looking at the image for a few minutes, we could improve it slightly with one more, simple step. From Image < Adjustments, select Brightness and Contrast. Increase the Contrast just slightly. This subtle step brings up

FIGURE 21.30   The image after applying Blur using the Smart Filter.

FIGURE 21.31   Applying just a hint of noise to the entire image.

the saturation of the color slightly and adds some sparkle to the painting. We are now finally finished (Figure 21.33). ♣

FIGURE 21.32 The finished painting?

FIGURE 21.33 The real finished painting after adding a bit of Brightness and Contrast.

CONCLUSION

Well, there you have it: the complete painting from sketch to finish. The goal was to paint a texturally complex image that would look more time-consuming than it was. We wanted something that would engage viewers and let them fill in the majority of the details. We also wanted an image that was humorous but a touch creepy. In the next chapter, we will incorporate most of the techniques we have covered in the previous few chapters. We will be painting a monster image using a different working method where we start with no preconceived ideas and create the creature as we go.

PAINTING A MONSTER
FROM SCRATCH

In this chapter, we will be painting a picture that illustrates the "less is more" concept. Basically, we want to create an image that looks like we spent a lot more time on it than we actually did. Unlike the previous chapters, we are not going to base this project on an existing sketch but start completely from scratch. This may entail some backing up and changing course as we experiment. It will also necessitate some modifications in the working procedure because there is not a solid idea of where the image is headed. Never fear, though, since this is often a fun way to work. I would not recommend this style of creating art, though, when you have deadlines involved or when you must please a client. This method of painting is most suited to painting for the sheer pleasure.

WHAT YOU NEED TO KNOW ABOUT PHOTOSHOP FOR THIS CHAPTER

The following tutorial assumes that you know some fundamentals of working in Photoshop CS3, such as:

- Where individual palettes are located
- How to adjust a brush's opacity
- How to create layers, how to change their Blending mode, and how to use layer styles
- How to resize your brush and sample color from within the image (preferably using the hot keys)
- How to create and use patterns
- How to create brushes

You can arrange the Photoshop workspace to suit your own liking, so this chapter does not discuss where to locate specific items.

TUTORIAL 22.1   PAINTING THE IMAGE

When you're ready to start painting the monster, follow these steps:

1. Unlike earlier chapters, there is not a scan of a sketch to start with, so this will be quite a bit different. The image that will evolve from this chapter will be more original and individual than those from the other chapters. Remember that every image without small red arrows indicating areas of special focus or images that are obviously close-ups represents a saved version of the image. You cannot save enough, so don't hesitate to save constantly. You will be happy in the end that you have gotten into this habit.

FIGURE 22.1   The basic scribble used to start the painting.

2. Create a new image in Photoshop that is approximately 800 × 800 pixels. We start with a smaller image just to make the initial sketching fast and easy. Over the course of the painting, we will increase the size of the image gradually as we refine the painting. If you want, open Figure 22.1 and skip to Step 3. Create a new layer. On the new layer, using the Airbrush Hard Round brush, begin to randomly scribble. What we are doing is looking for a starting place. Quite often shapes and ideas will arise out of a scribbled image as your brain becomes less engaged in trying to draw a recognizable shape. The only pre-conceived idea should be that you are painting some type of creature. At this point, do not try to narrow anything down, such as this will be based on a reptile, bird, or anything recognizable. The point is to stay open to your brain's inner eye. The image develops, and I can start to see a head, so going with the flow, I indicate a couple areas where there are eyes and a mouth using some smaller brush strokes (Figure 22.2). Usually, when working this way, we would start with a larger brush and decrease the size as our mind's eye begins to see shapes.

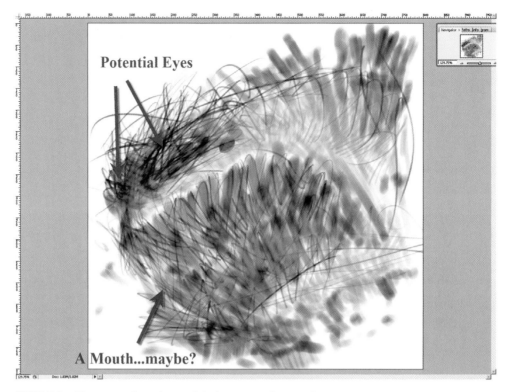

FIGURE 22.2 The areas where there might be eyes and a mouth.

3. We will be able to see the image better and use both light and dark strokes as we develop the idea if we are not drawing on white, so, using the Paint Bucket tool, fill the background with a mid-value and fairly neutral color. Continue to scribble and draw on the image layer, but now using both light and dark strokes. Figure 22.3 shows the scribbled image with a darker background. In this image, we want to create something that is dark and creepy, and our goal is to let the viewer's eye fill in many of the details, so drawing on a darker background is perfect. When you have something you like, save the image.

4. To help us see the image a bit better with more contrast, duplicate the layer with the drawing on it. The shapes and strokes are much clearer now (Figure 22.4). Save the image again.

5. Now is the time for some serious experimentation. Create four or five additional layers, and using the large texture brushes in the book.abr brushes, stamp some large textures over the image. Put only one stamp on each layer. If not already loaded, the brush library, the book.abr brushes is located on the CD-ROM. You should either replace the standard Photoshop

ON THE CD

FIGURE 22.3   The scribbled image with a darker background.

FIGURE 22.4   To see the image better with more contrast, duplicate the drawing layer.

brushes with this library or append the currently loaded brushes with this group. Figure 22.5 shows the original image duplicated several times with different textures over each duplicate. This image is only an example, and you should just stamp the textures on individual layers.

FIGURE 22.5 The original image duplicated several times with different textures over each duplicate.

6. Turn each layer on or off singly and in combination with other layers to find a good combination that adds a grungy feel to the drawing. Use the opacity of the grungy layer to lessen the texture some. We do not want the texture to overpower our drawing but to help add more detail and a bit of randomness to the image. Merge the drawing and grungy texture layers together. Do not merge the drawing with the background (Figure 22.6). We are starting to get a dark and creepy image suggesting a monster. Save the image.

7. Create a new layer under the drawing layer. On this new layer, use the airbrush brushes and start to paint some color into the painting. Around the mouth some red is painted, and some green is painted on the back of the head. Figure 22.7 shows the image with the added color. The color also helps darken the image a little, adding a bit more mystery to the whole thing.

8. Make the whole thing much darker by changing the Blend mode of the drawing layer from Normal to Multiply. The results are shown in Figure 22.8. Save the image.

FIGURE 22.6   A dark and creepy image is beginning to emerge.

FIGURE 22.7   Adding some color to the image.

9. Using the same brush, begin to paint some teeth with more detail on a new layer above the drawing (Figure 22.9). Use only black and white at this point and do not add any color. We will add some color in the next step, but for now the teeth shapes and values are what are important. When the teeth are looking right, save the image.

FIGURE 22.8 The whole image is made darker by changing the Blend mode of the drawing layer from Normal to Multiply.

FIGURE 22.9 Painting some teeth.

10. To add some color to the teeth, create two new layers above the teeth layer. Load a selection from the teeth layer using the Select > Load Selection command (Figure 22.10).
11. On the bottom of the two new layers, with the selection active, fill the selection with a light cream color as in Figure 22.11.

FIGURE 22.10   Creating a selection from the teeth layer.

FIGURE 22.11   Filling the selection on a new layer with a creamy color.

12. Change the Blending mode of this layer to Soft Light (Figure 22.12).

FIGURE 22.12 Changing the Blending mode to Soft Light.

13. Load the selection again, and, on the top new layer, fill the selection with a bright orange-red color (Figure 22.13).
14. Change the Blending mode of the orange-red layer to Soft Light also. The image should now look something like Figure 22.14. Everything is looking so dark and messy that we begin to wonder if we have ruined the image before we have really started. This is a common feeling with artists, and you should not worry if you feel this way now. With a little luck and some hard work, we will pull this image out of the fire and have a great painting at the end of the day.
15. Switch to the Eraser tool and carefully erase on both layers until the teeth of the monster look like the ones in Figure 22.15. This needs to be a careful and delicate process. We want to have the majority of the red colors on the edges of the teeth and the choppers themselves a kind of creamy to white color. It is now safe to merge all the head layers without the background into one layer. If you would rather keep the layers just in case they are

FIGURE 22.13   Fill the selection on the top layer with a bright red-orange color.

FIGURE 22.14   Change the Blending mode to Soft Light on this layer, too.

needed again in the future, then hide the background layer and hold down the following keys: Shift+Ctrl+Alt+e. This will take all the layers and combine them into a new layer. Make sure to save another copy of the image.

FIGURE 22.15 Erasing on both layers until the teeth are realized.

16. Using various brushes and some dark colors, paint some more random strokes over the character (Figure 22.16). Save the image.

FIGURE 22.16 Adding more texture and random strokes to the creature.

17. It is time to enlarge the image in anticipation of adding a body to the large mouth we have painted. Select the background and from the Image menu pick Canvas Size. An options window pops up. Change the width to 2,400 pixels wide. Click the middle of the first row of Anchor boxes. This will add all the new width to the right of the current image. Leave everything else default and click OK (Figure 22.17).

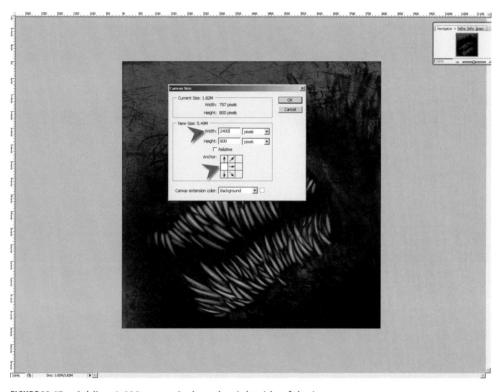

FIGURE 22.17   Adding 1,600 more pixels to the right side of the image.

18. The new image has a lot more space on the right to add a body to the monster, as you can see in Figure 22.18.
19. Using much the same type of process as went into the head, we will now draw in some basic shapes to start to develop a body for the creature. Using a lot of scribbling and working on a new layer that is below the head layer, paint in the beginning shapes. Remember that we are not settled on any particular shape or creature, so these strokes should be pretty random. Figure 22.19 shows some of the first painted strokes. Save the image when you are satisfied with what is being painted.

FIGURE 22.18   The new image now measures 800 pixels high by 2,400 pixels wide.

FIGURE 22.19   The beginnings of a body to the monster.

20. Merge the head and new body layer together. Move the new layer created when merging the two layers more toward the center of the image to give some room on the left of the creature's head (Figure 22.20).

FIGURE 22.20   Move the monster layer into the center of the image to have more room to paint on the left side of the figure.

21. Using the same brushes, go wild painting the body. We have started to add areas that have scales. There are some dark red stains under the teeth. Areas that loosely resemble claws and some that may be bony spikes coming from the back are visible in Figure 22.21. There is no right or wrong approach at this stage.

FIGURE 22.21   Go wild painting in some more body.

22. We need some more room at the bottom of the image, so using the same procedure as before, add an additional 400 pixels to the bottom. When the image has been resized, continue to paint in the creature. Some green indications of eyes have been added to the head areas along with some large eyebrows or ears. You can see the results in Figure 22.22. Save the image.

FIGURE 22.22   Some eyes have been added to the creature.

23. Continue to develop the creature. We will start to work into the background with some color to establish the ground. Spines, bones, claws, and other features are starting to become more distinct in appearance. The eyes have been further refined, and it turns out this creature has six. Some areas will become less distinct, while others will be refined. At this point we really should have a vision of where the monster is heading. Figure 22.23 shows the entire painting at this stage of development.

FIGURE 22.23   After adding more details to the image.

24. Figure 22.24 shows a close-up of the creature's head and face.
25. The scales and spines on the back of the monster are painted back into the image as shown in Figure 22.25.
26. Continue painting with multiple brushes and add more dimensional details into the figure, as shown in Figure 22.26. Some bloody spots are added below the teeth. We decide to let the front claws disappear into a gloomy foreground. On a new layer, a cracked pattern is stamped and painted to give a fantasy feeling to the whole image. Some details are best left to the imagination, so the claws are only indicated against the light sky. A slight glow is given to the green eyes. We add more detail to the figure, generally using the Airbrush Pen Opacity Flow brush in smaller sizes, trying to maintain a random feel. Now, this is not real detail but is simply letting the textures already present suggest detail. Finish work is done in the mouth area. At this stage, the image is for all intents and purposes finished.
27. Let's add one last touch to the monster before calling him done. Create a new layer and carefully paint a long string of drool flipping out of the monster's mouth. This adds the illusion of motion, as if the monster is turning

FIGURE 22.24   A close-up of the head of the monster.

FIGURE 22.25   Scales and spines are repainted on the creature's back.

FIGURE 22.26   The finishing details are added to the painting.

around quickly to face the viewer. When you are happy with the drool, merge all the layers into one image and save the file. Figure 22.27 shows the finished painting.

FIGURE 22.27   Adding a bit of drool for that small but so important final touch.

CONCLUSION

Well, there you have it: the complete painting from scribble to finish. The goal was to paint a texturally complex image that would look more time-consuming than it was. We wanted something that would engage viewers and let them fill in the majority of the details with their minds. We also wanted an image that was dark and creepy looking. In the next chapter, we will incorporate many of the techniques we have covered in the last few chapters. We will be painting a nerdy character with his ray gun invention.

PAINTING THE PROFESSOR IMAGE

The tutorial in this chapter is different from any other in this book. Here, we show the whole process from sketch to final image, including all the back-tracking, changes of mind, and errors made while the image was painted. The style of this image is also more illustration than painting, meaning there will be many more stylized touches such as outlines and flat areas of color than I would generally use in a digital painting.

All of the work in this image was done in Photoshop CS3.

WHAT YOU NEED TO KNOW ABOUT PHOTOSHOP FOR THIS CHAPTER

The following tutorial assumes that you know some fundamentals of working in Photoshop CS, such as:

- Where individual palettes are located
- How to adjust a brush's opacity
- How to use the Filter Gallery and the Liquify filter
- How to create layers and change their Blending mode when needed
- How to resize your brush and sample color from within the image (preferably using the hot keys)
- How to create patterns
- How to create brushes

You can arrange the Photoshop workspace to suit your own liking, so this chapter does not discuss where to locate specific items.

| TUTORIAL 23.1 | **PAINTING THE PROFESSOR IMAGE** |

When you're ready to start, follow these steps:

ON THE CD

1. Scan a sketch at 300 dpi. Doing so will give you a large enough image for decent prints. The original sketch I scanned (shown in Figure 23.1) is available on the CD-ROM if you care to use it instead of a sketch of your own.
2. We are going to make a few adjustments to the image before we start painting it. First, let's cut and paste the entire image back into itself. Select the whole image using Ctrl+a or Select All from the Select menu. Cut the image using Ctrl+x or Cut from the Edit menu and Paste what is cut back into the workspace using the Ctrl+v keys or Paste from the Edit menu. Now, we have the sketch on a new layer above a white background. Using the Polygonal Lasso tool, select the head from the chin up. Cut and Paste the head back into the image on a new layer. Select the shoulders and upper arms of the sketch on the first layer and Cut and Paste them back into the image creating a new layer when you do. Use Edit > Free Transform or the keys Ctrl+t to access the

FIGURE 23.1   The original sketch.

Free Transform command and give the head a bit of tilt. Using the same command, give the shoulders a bit of tilt in the opposite direction. Figure 23.2 shows the head and shoulders tilted slightly, revealing the white background.

FIGURE 23.2   The head and shoulders tilted slightly, revealing the white background.

When you get the amount of tilt you want, go ahead and Flatten the image merging all the layers. Don't worry about the white showing through because we are going to get rid of it. Using the Levels command found under Image > Adjustments, move the dark and light slider points until most of the gray background is gone as in Figure 23.3. There will still be some small spots visible, but these are not important.

FIGURE 23.3 The gray background is gone after using the Levels command.

Duplicate the sketch layer several times. Use the Filter > Liquify filter to vary the character to a greater or lesser degree. I made the eyes slightly larger and cheeks a bit thinner. Figure 23.4 shows the difference between the original sketch on the left and my tweaked version on the right.

3. Crop the sketch a bit in preparation for painting. Figure 23.5 is the sketch we will now start painting on. This file is available on the CD-ROM for you to use should you want to.

ON THE CD

FIGURE 23.4   A comparison of the original and the tweaked version of the sketch.

FIGURE 23.5   Crop the sketch a bit in preparation for painting.

4. Just when we have cropped the image, I now decide that it needs more space on the right side for a longer barrel on the gun he is holding. Using Canvas Size found under the Image menu, add 500 pixels to the right side of the image (Figure 23.6). Save the image. Always remember to save the image whenever a large change has been made. Try to save images in a numerical sequence so you can go back to an earlier image if you make a large mistake or just decide to change direction with the painting.

FIGURE 23.6 Add 500 pixels to the right side of the image.

5. Create a new layer and redraw the gun barrel, making it longer. When you have something you like, erase the original drawing underneath and merge the two layers together (Figure 23.7). Save again. You get the idea here that saving is very important. You can assume from this point on that we have saved every image displayed in this demonstration to its individual file.

FIGURE 23.7   Redraw the gun barrel making it longer.

6. Duplicate the sketch layer and change its Blending mode to Multiply. Everything that was white will now be transparent. Create a new layer and drag it under the Multiply sketch layer. Using the Sketcher Soft brush, paint in a rough background color. Do not try to make the layer nice and smooth. Switch brushes to the Airbrush Pen Opacity Flow brush and paint in the figure's colors (Figure 23.8).

7. While all the layers are visible, hold down the following key combination Shift+Ctrl+Alt+e. All the layers are merged into one layer while maintaining the original separate layers. Use this often when experimenting with different techniques. With the new layer active, go to the Filter menu and select Filter Gallery. Experiment as much as you want to layer different effects. Figure 23.9 shows the Cutout and Watercolor filters that are used to create the look in the image preview.

Click OK when done. Figure 23.10 shows the image with the Filter Gallery applied. Make sure to save the work at this point.

FIGURE 23.8   Painting in the background and figure's colors.

FIGURE 23.9   The Filter Gallery.

FIGURE 23.10   The image with the Filter Gallery effects applied.

8. Create a new layer. Fill the new layer with White. Double-click on the layer in the Layer palette to open the Layer Styles options. Check the Pattern Overlay box. Select the Speckles pattern from the palette of different patterns. Leave everything else default and click OK (Figure 23.11).

9. Change the Blending mode of the new layer to Multiply. Click on the Eye icon just to the left of Effects below the layer (Figure 23.12).
   The layer becomes transparent except for lots of small speckles covering the entire image. Your painting should now look like Figure 23.13. Save the image. Flatten the image and Save As, giving it a new name.

10. Pick the Airbrush Pen Opacity Flow brush, use a mid-value for both Opacity and Flow, and begin painting your image. Use a technique where you are not trying to blend much. Imagine that you are painting a "Paint by Number" image and try to fill in distinct shapes with individual colors. Of course, there will be some subtle blending as the strokes overlap each other, and this is fine. Figure 23.14 shows a close-up of the character's face with the color being applied. Do not try to cover all of the drawing, and notice how distinct each color is being applied.

FIGURE 23.11   A new layer about to be overlaid on the painting.

FIGURE 23.12   The layer becomes transparent.

FIGURE 23.13   The painting with the speckled layer applied.

FIGURE 23.14   A close-up of the character's face.

11. Continue to use the same brush and start to work down the character onto the lab coat. We are sampling colors mostly from within the image at this point and not going back to the color palette except when a very bright or

different color is needed. Figure 23.15 shows the whole image as we start to work down from the face. It is important to notice that background colors are also being used as we paint up to the contours of the character. Using both foreground and background colors in tandem helps keep the contours clean and manageable.

FIGURE 23.15   The whole image as we start to work down from the face.

12. We decide to make a major change at this point and modify the rifle to look more like a ray gun. Create a new layer and change the end of the barrel to look more science fiction–like and a bit goofy. When you have something you like, merge the character and rifle barrel layers together. Continue to paint down the character and the ray gun, blocking in the colors very simply (Figure 23.16).

13. Continue to refine the shapes of the ray gun, lab coat, and pants. Zoom in on the face and paint the eyes in the glasses. Paint the eyes like the glass lenses are magnifying the iris, making them appear much too large for a realistic face. Do this to add a bit of humor and play on the stereotype of the mad scientist wearing very thick glasses. Add some bright greens to the top of the energy pack he is wearing over his shoulder to represent the glow of the nuclear material being used to power the ray gun. Paint some more details on the pens in the pocket protector. Figure 23.17 shows our progress to this point, and while we are painting carefully, do not worry about painting in lots of details at this time.

FIGURE 23.16   Paint down the character and the ray gun, blocking in the colors very simply.

FIGURE 23.17   The painting to this point.

14. Continue painting until you are nearing the completion of the character. We have painted the ray gun, finished the lab coat, and completed the energy pack, complete with straps holding the thing to the character's back. Add some strong highlights to the glasses to make them look like they have glass lenses (Figure 23.18).

FIGURE 23.18   Strong highlights are added to the glasses.

15. Overall, things in the image are moving along nicely, but there is a problem. The ray gun looks pretty flat. To give it more dimension, we are going to use a trick to quickly add some darks where appropriate. Use the Polygonal Lasso tool and make a rough selection around the ray gun. Copy and Paste the selection. There is now a new layer containing the ray gun only. Change the Blending mode of the new layer to Multiply. Everything goes very dark, which is exactly what we want. Move the opacity slider down to about 54%. Now things are still dark but not quite as jarring. Using the Eraser tool, carefully erase the areas on the new layer that you want to be lighter, leaving only the darks. After a bit of careful erasing, you now have a ray gun that has more dimension and depth (Figure 23.19). Save the image and merge the layers. Save again.

FIGURE 23.19   Adding shadows to the ray gun.

ON THE CD

16. We want to increase the "nerd" feeling of the character. What better way to do this than give him some plaid pants? Open the file plaids.psd. This file is a multi-layer Photoshop file with a different plaid pattern on each layer and is available on the CD-ROM. Decide which plaid to use and hide the layers above it. It really does not matter which pattern we go with. From the Edit menu, select Define Pattern. A dialog box appears with a thumbnail of your new pattern and a suggested name. Name the pattern or use the default suggestion. Close the plaid psd file. On the painting, use a selection tool and select the pants. Create a new layer and, with the selection still active, fill this selection with the new plaid pattern. Reduce the Opacity of the layer to around 85% so you can just see the painted image underneath. Your image will look something like Figure 23.20, depending on the plaid pattern chosen. It looks better but is pretty flat and lifeless.

FIGURE 23.20   A plaid pattern overlaid on the pants.

17. Create another layer on top of the plaid layer. Select Load Selection from the transparency of the plaid layer. Select the new layer and fill the active selection with a mid-value gray. Change the Blending mode of the new layer to Multiply and, using the Eraser tool, erase everything but the shadows on the plaid pants. Now the plaid pants have a lot more form, and the image will look similar to Figure 23.21.

18. Merge all the layers together. Figure 23.22 shows the entire painting with the new and improved plaid pants.

19. Using the Airbrush Pen Opacity Flow brush, paint in some glowing green light on the edges of the character's face. This gives the impression that his energy pack is generating light and adds some nice complementary colors to the oranges in the hair and skin (Figure 23.23).

20. Add a glowing red light on top of the ray gun (Figure 23.24).

21. We want to add some glow and smoke to the end of the ray gun to give the impression that it has been recently fired. Before we do this, though, we want to darken the right side of the image so there will be contrast between

FIGURE 23.21   Giving some dimension to the plaid pants.

FIGURE 23.22   The image with the finished plaid pants.

FIGURE 23.23   Adding some glowing green light to the edge of the face.

FIGURE 23.24   Adding glow to the red button on the ray gun.

the smoke, glow, and background. To darken the right side of the image, we will use a layer mask. Duplicate the layer and change its Blending mode to Multiply. The entire image becomes darker. Click on the Layer Mask icon at the bottom of the Layers palette. Fill the new Layer Mask with a linear gradient from black on the left to white on the right. Notice how there is a nice even transition from light on the left to dark on the right. Use a brush to paint black on the layer mask over the entire character. Look at the thumbnail in image 23.25 if you need to see an example.

FIGURE 23.25   Painting on the layer mask.

Now there is a nice gradation across the background from lighter on the left to darker on the right while the character stays the same value as the original layer (Figure 23.26). Save the image and merge all the layers.

22. Let's make the tip of the ray gun glow like it has been fired. First, duplicate the layer so you are not working on the original. Pick the Airbrush Soft Round 300 brush and change its Mode to Color Dodge. Lower the Opacity and Flow of the brush to around 30% each for more control when painting. Choose a bright red-orange in the color palette and lightly paint over the tip or the ray gun. Change colors occasionally to more red or yellow and paint until you have a nicely glowing tip of the gun (Figure 23.27).

FIGURE 23.26   A nice gradation across the background from lighter on the left to darker on the right.

FIGURE 23.27   A nicely glowing tip of the ray gun.

There are additional areas where we can use this technique within the image. Anything that is supposed to be glowing is a prime candidate. Paint the same effect on the glowing light on top of the gun scope, the glowing light on top of the antennae on the energy pack, and the green nuclear materials (Figure 23.28).

FIGURE 23.28   Adding a glow to the green nuclear materials.

23. Let's add a bit more contrast to the entire image. Duplicate the image layer and change its Blending mode to Multiply. Lower the opacity until there is just a slight increase in the contrast of the image. Doing this also adds a bit more saturation to the bright colors (Figure 23.29).

24. We will now add some smoke curling up from the tip of the gun. This is an easy step but will add a lot of visual appeal to the image. Create a new layer to paint the smoke on. Using the Soft Mechanical 48 Pixel brush with Opacity set to 70% and Flow to about 50%, paint a curling trail of smoke using a slightly gray color on the new layer. Try to give the stroke a nice random feeling like it is smoke rising slowly into the air (Figure 23.30).

FIGURE 23.29 Adding a bit more contrast to the entire image.

FIGURE 23.30 The smoke rising from the ray gun painted on a new layer.

25. The smoke is not done. Duplicate the smoke layer twice. Pick the bottom smoke layer to make it active. From Filters apply a Gaussian blur. We want enough blur to soften the smoke but not completely destroy its curving nature. Select the top smoke layer and use the Liquify filter to give this smoke a very random and snaky appearance. With all three smoke layers visible, we have a stylized but quite convincing wisp of smoke rising from the end of the gun barrel. Select all three of the smoke layers and merge them together (Figure 23.31). Save your image.

FIGURE 23.31   Merging the three layers of smoke together.

26. Use the technique described above to add the glow to the gun barrel to add some glow to the smoke. Create a new layer and paint some subtle glow around the smoke (Figure 23.32). Merge all the layers and save the image once again.

27. One last step and we are done with the ray gun. Once again create a new layer and using the Airbrush07 brush stamp a few sparkles around the tip of the gun barrel with a bright yellow-orange color. Change the Blending mode to Color Dodge and adjust the Opacity of the layer to taste (Figure 23.33).

28. One more thing to do and we are done with the painting. We are going to add just a bit of noise to the image. We will do this for several reasons: First, adding some noise will help the image look a bit more organic and not quite

FIGURE 23.32 Creating a glow to the smoke.

FIGURE 23.33 Stamp with the brush a few sparkles around the tip of the gun barrel with a bright yellow-orange color.

as digital, and, second, adding some noise will build on the technique we have used by leaving speckles in the background. It will help unify the overall feeling of the painting. Create a new layer just in case there are any problems or mistakes. On the new layer, create some noise using the Add Noise filter located in the Filter > Add Noise menu. We only want subtle noise, so move the Amount slider down to about 4.8%. The preview window will let us see the results if you have it checked. Figure 23.34 shows the Add Noise interface and a close-up of our character with noise previewed over him.

FIGURE 23.34   Adding a bit of noise to the image.

29. We are now finished with our painting, and you can see the results in Figure 23.35.

FIGURE 23.35   The finished painting.

CONCLUSION

This is one of the more complicated digital paintings that we have attempted. It may not end up being a good painting, but you will have learned a great deal while doing it. The image of the Professor is the last demonstration in the book because it's important to show the complete process of digital painting, including the mistakes and explorations that go into creating an image. We hope that seeing the entire process will spur your own experimentation and help eliminate any fear you may have of trying something new.

A

ABOUT THE CD-ROM

Chapter 11 folder: Contains the image used in the example demonstrated in Chapter 11.

Chapter 12 folder: Contains three different texture images that are used in the examples demonstrated in Chapter 12.

Chapter 13 folder: Contains the texture used in the chapter to demonstrate the use of a texture in making a Photoshop brush.

Chapter 17 folder: Contains the original sketch, which is used in the demonstration.

Chapter 18 folder: Contains the original sketch to use when following the tutorial. Also contains two custom brush libraries used in the tutorial and two custom swatch palettes to use in your own projects.

Chapter 19 folder: Contains the original sketch used as the basis of the painting as well as crosshatch.tif, which is the basis for making your own pattern file.

Chapter 20 folder: Contains the original sketch used in the Chapter 20 tutorial painting.

Chapter 21 folder: Contains the original sketch used in the tutorial.

Chapter 23 folder: Contains the original sketch used in the painting and the file plaids.psd.

Brushes folder: Contains all of the custom brushes and more in their rough state that were used in the painting tutorials of each chapter. These brushes are compatible for both the Mac and PC.

Textures folder: Contains 210 different textures for you to experiment with when making your own pattern and brush files. A subfolder called Reptile Textures contains 32 reptile skin textures.

Patterns folder: Contains the dons patterns file that is used in projects throughout the book.

Extras folder: Contains a couple of extra files that can be used when making art. There is also a short movie showing the painting of a face. There is no sound, and it is done in an older version of Photoshop, but it might be of some interest to you.

WHAT IS PHOTOSHOP?

Photoshop is the premiere digital imaging tool available. Additional information can be found at

www.adobe.com
Toll-Free Number
800-833-6687

U.S. and Canadian customers can get recorded information about how to order products, determine the status of an order, or contact a customer service representative at the San Jose Corporate Headquarters:

Adobe Systems Inc.
345 Park Avenue
San Jose, California 95110-2704
Tel: 408-536-6000
Fax: 408-537-6000

If you have any trouble installing or using the demonstration, please contact Adobe Technical Support at *http://www.adobe.com/support/*.

It is hoped that you will find something of use and pleasure when using the CD-ROM.

SYSTEM REQUIREMENTS

Windows

- Intel Pentium III or 4 processor
- Microsoft Windows 2000 with Service Pack 3 or Windows XP
- 192 MB RAM
- 280 MB of available hard disk space
- Color monitor with 16-bit color or greater video card

- 1,024 × 768 or greater resolution
- CD-ROM drive
- Internet or phone connection required for product activation

Macintosh

- PowerPC G3, G4, or G5 processor
- Mac OS X v.10.2.4 through v.10.3 with Java Runtime Environment 1.4
- 192 MB RAM
- 320 MB of available hard disk space
- 1,024 × 768 or greater resolution
- CD-ROM drive

INDEX

403